Table of Content

Introduction to Google Apps

Google Apps (formerly, Google Apps for Your Domain) is an integrated suite of Google applications that includes an email program, a WYSIWYG webpage editor, an online calendar, an instant messaging client with voice capabilities, and a web-based word processor cum spreadsheet software.

Business organizations, educational institutions, and even individuals (like you and me) can use the Google Apps service for free (though a premier edition is also available). And since Google Apps require little or no technical expertise, it may be a blessing for small business owners who have little or no budget for IT.

The various components of Google Apps (like calendar, email, spreadsheet, word processor, etc) are hosted on Google servers and so the end users are saved from the hassles of installing or upgrading software at their end. Administrators can access and manage user accounts through a web-based control panel.

The virtual collaboration features of Google Docs are far superior and user-friendly than what is currently offered by Microsoft Office applications. To get started with Google Apps, you'll need a web domain name. Recently, Google partnered with registrars, Go Daddy and eNom, to sell domain names at $10/year. Domains bought through Google come bundled with Google Apps requiring no configuration by the owners. The downside is that India specific domains like .in or .co.in cannot be purchased via Google yet, though they can still be integrated with Google Apps.

If you are planning to use an existing web domain with Google Apps, just make sure that you have access to your DNS settings, which is generally available with the domain host. Google Apps is available in two flavors – the standard (aka free) edition and a premier (aka paid) edition. The premier edition subscribers are given 10GB of email storage space (as opposed to 2GB+ in the free edition) and a 99.9% uptime guarantee for email. Other premium facilities include access to 24/7 support by phone, the ability to hide all contextual advertisements on Google services, and several advanced features tailored for the enterprise.

The premier edition doesn't come cheap it costs a whopping $50 per user account per year - but the good news is that most families, business owners, and individuals will be quite content with the offerings of the standard edition because, except for telephone support and small inboxes, Google is providing the same applications in both the editions.

Google Apps service is a runaway success and much of that can be attributed to Gmail, the web-based email program of Google. In an era when 86% of all email messages that hit our inboxes are spam, Gmail is equipped with some of the best spam filtering algorithms that have proved to be very effective in keeping spam out of our mailboxes.

Google Docs & Spreadsheets is another useful application bundled with Google Apps that may change the way you write and share documents with co-workers and clients. Think of it as an online version of Microsoft Word or Excel software the look n' feel and features are quite similar to Microsoft software except that you compose documents inside a web browser and data is stored online (on Google servers) so it can be accessed from any computer that is connected to the internet.

Google Docs & Spreadsheets is tightly integrated with GTalk, the instant messaging client from Google. Workers in various locations can edit the same document/spreadsheet simultaneously – they can open a chat window and discuss /review changes made by other authors in real-time.

Google Apps for Education is a cloud computing package. It provides access to products powered by Google but administered by your organization. Doing so, the school accepts the responsibility of how the services are used by their end-users, as well as for the data stored. By providing organizations with control, schools are given the power to easily create and manage both staff and student accounts.

In many respects, Google Apps replicates the basic functionalities of Microsoft Office. The difference though is that it allows collaboration and sharing at the click of a button anywhere, any time.

Examples of The Activities In Which You Can Use Google Apps:

Planning & Organisation: Unlike having a document on a projector with everyone watching on, Google Apps provides a means for everyone to work together in real-time.

Data Collection: Although Google Sheets does not have all of the intricacies of Google Sheets, it allows for quite a bit. From gathering test results to collecting data, there are many different possibilities for sharing and sorting.

Goals And Portfolios: Using Google allows students and teachers to collaborate in regards to supporting goals and maintaining a digital portfolio of work.

Feedback: Whether it be adding a comment, filling out an exit ticket, or completing the pre-test, Google Apps provides many ways to gain and give feedback.

Templates: Although most simply make copies of files, Google Apps also allows you to create templates that the whole organization can then access.

Integration: Individual Google programs and services can talk to other popular programs. For example, Google Docs lets you import and export Excel and OpenOffice Calc spreadsheets. And if your company is thinking of making the switch to Google Apps, integration with your existing IT infrastructure is possible (not a no-brainer, to be sure, but well within reach of any firm that has one tech-savvy person and this book). For example, you can migrate email from your current mail server into Google Apps Email while preserving messages' date information, read/unread status, and the filing system people have used to organize their messages.

Updates And Bug Fixes: Do you dread having to download and install program updates and patches because of the havoc they sometimes wreak on your system? Well, say goodbye to that sinking feeling. Since Google applications are on the Web, Google automatically takes care of updates and bug fixes for you.

Many of the queries and questions about Google Apps relate to the internet and ease of access. However, these concerns can be overcome by setting up offline access by downloading the Google Drive application and opening documents through Chrome. Although you are unable to work collaboratively with them, you are also able to edit Microsoft documents.

Chapter 1: Google Apps

What Is Google Apps?

Google Apps is a suite of web-based messaging and collaboration applications that Google hosts on its servers. Google provides these applications as a "service," rather than as software to download and install. To access these applications, you simply use a web browser on a computer that's connected to the Internet.

What Does Google Apps Mean?

Google Apps is a Web-based and collaborative Software as a Service (SaaS) solution that customizes the proprietary Google platform and brand for businesses of all sizes, including large enterprises. Google Apps facilitates the provisioning of Google applications and user/enterprise management tools, including Gmail, Google Talk, Google Calendar, Google Docs, Google Videos, and Google Cloud Connect.

Google Apps

Google Apps is backed by the same infrastructure and resources provided by the standard Google services. It features 99.9 percent uptime availability, administrative support, and other corporate support features explicitly described in the Google Apps Service

Level Agreement (SLA). Google Apps customizes applications for different industries, as described below:

- ❖ **Google Apps (Free):** Gmail (up to ten free email accounts), Google Calendar, Google Sites, and Google Docs
- ❖ **Google Apps For Education:** Free applications for schools
- ❖ **Google Apps For Business:** Paid version, which provides Web-based application tools for collaboration
- ❖ **Google Apps For Government:** Web-based and government certified collaboration tools
- ❖ **Google Apps For Nonprofit:** Collaboration and communication tools for U.S. nonprofit organizations

Why Google Apps?

Many factors contributed to our decision to "go Google." Increasing license fees and the complexities of operating the past Novell GroupWise system meant escalating costs and risk. The recent budget crisis combined with the projected growth of the University required us to find a more effective and cost-efficient solution. Much higher education institutions have proven that Google Apps have been a solution and to a large extent, that has been proven here at Georgia Southern with the successful implementation of students and preliminary testing by staff and faculty volunteers.

More Specifically, Google Apps Provides:

- ❖ Lower infrastructure costs
- ❖ All your email is stored securely on Google's servers, so we'll no longer need to maintain email servers on-site.
- ❖ Ability to further consolidate email platforms
- ❖ Lower support costs
- ❖ Because Google hosts the email and calendar services, there's no more email client software to maintain on your computer.

Innovative Solutions: We can leverage the powerful collaboration tools of the Google Apps platform to provide the University community with easy-to-use tools for sharing information and getting work done efficiently.

Highly Scalable Environment: With Google Apps, our email capacity continues to grow automatically as Georgia Southern grows, and we avoid many complexities, risks, and future costs.

Access To Services From Anywhere, Anytime: Google Apps are designed to operate in cyberspace and is functional with any computer or mobile device with an Internet connection, anywhere in the world;

Security And Survivability: Google's security resources are world-class and far outpace the resources that any single higher education institution could ever provide. Google Apps offers a strong and extensive security infrastructure that has passed the American Institute of Certified Public Accountants Statement on Auditing Standard 70. Google data centers provide redundancy of services and duplication of data across large geographical areas making them resilient to common disaster scenarios.

State Of The Art Features: With Google's next-generation applications, faculty, students, and staff operate in an environment of information collaboration. Google is constantly innovating new applications and capabilities. Google also provides a programming interface that allows the University to create its Google-based applications.

What Exactly Do Google Apps Include?

Your new Google account does include the following services:

- ❖ Gmail "Google mail'
- ❖ Google Calendar
- ❖ GChat "Google Talk"
- ❖ Google Drive
- ❖ Google Sites

What Are The Key Benefits?

Lots Of Storage: You have a full 25 GB of online storage for your email, so you can archive all of your emails online. You do not need to worry about deleting messages or saving them in offline folders.

Enhanced Message Organization And Retrieval: With Google Mail, you spend less time managing folders and searching for messages. For example, you can add one or more tags, or "labels," to your messages to organize and store them more efficiently. And with the Google-powered search feature, you can find any message quickly and easily, whether it's in your Inbox or stored in your message archive.

Easier Calendar Sharing: Google Calendar lets you and your team members quickly and easily share your calendars and specify the details you want to show. Calendar sharing is a great way for you and your coworkers to keep each other informed about your schedules. Now it's easier than ever to find out if someone is in a meeting, on a business trip, or vacation.

Integrated Chat: With the Google Talk instant messaging application, you can communicate instantly with your coworkers right from the Email interface. Also, all your chats are automatically saved in your Email application, so you can always retrieve important information.

Real-Time Collaboration: Using Google Docs, you can create documents, spreadsheets, and presentations, and you and your team members can view and edit them at the same time. You can still use your Microsoft Office products as needed, but now you'll have more options for storing and collaborating on your documents.

Easy-To-Build Team Web Sites: With Google Sites, your team can quickly publish a robust internal web site on which to gather all sorts of shared information, such as documents, spreadsheets, presentations, files, and videos. You can even embed Google calendars and other gadgets on your site!

Top 10 Essential Google Apps For Every Android User

When you buy an Android smartphone, you are buying into a rich set of applications, services, and products from Google, the developer of the Android ecosystem. There is far more to Google than its search engine and operating system, it has you covered for most of your needs from navigation to cloud storage and email. Google's apps run better on Android. This is because Google and the Android operating system are so tightly intertwined. They're also easily accessible on your PC, irrespective of whether you are a MAC or Windows user. Alcatel has compiled a list of the must-have Google apps for every Android user:

1. Google

Find quick answers, explore your interests, and get a feed of updates on what matters to you. You can use the search engine for almost any question Google even responds invoice.

2. Google Play Music

Google Play Music features millions of songs for every taste and mood. Instantly start radio stations based on songs, artists, or albums, or browse by genre, mood, activity, decade, and more.

3. Google Docs

Google Docs allows you to create, edit, and collaborate with others on documents from your Android phone or tablet. Never worry about losing your work everything is saved automatically as you type.

4. Maps Navigation & Transport

Going somewhere? Go with Maps, the official Map app, that gives you real-time GPS navigation, traffic, and details about millions of businesses, including reviews and popular times.

5. Google Drive

Store your files in Google Drive and access them from any smartphone, tablet, or computer. Files in Drive such as your videos, photos, and documents – are backed up safely. You can invite people to view, edit, or leave comments on your files or folders.

6. Waze GPS, Maps, Traffic Alerts & Sat Nav

Waze tells you about traffic, construction, police, accidents, and more in real-time. If traffic is bad on your route, Waze will change your route to save you time. Waze gives you real-time updates based on other users' input.

7. Gmail

Gmail is an easy-to-use email app that saves you time and keeps your messages safe. Instantly receive your messages via push notifications, read and respond online or offline and find any message quickly.

8. Clock

Clock combines the functionality you need into one simple, beautiful package.

- ❖ Set alarms, add timers and run a stopwatch
- ❖ Keep track of time around the world using the World Clock
- ❖ Pair with Android Wear devices to bring your alarms and timers to your wrist.

9. Google Keep Notes And Lists

Google Keep makes it easy to capture a thought or list for yourself, and also allows you to share it with friends and family. Record a voice memo on the go and have it automatically transcribed. Snap a photo of a poster, receipt, or document and easily organize or find it later in search.

10. Gboard – The Google Keyboard

Gboard has everything you love about Google Keyboard – speed and reliability, Glide Typing, voice typing, and more – plus Google Search built-in. Search Google while you have your keyboard open – which means no need to switch between apps.

Advantages Of Google Apps

1. Administering Google Apps Is Easy

The admin interface is dead-simple to use, and pretty self-explanatory. Everything you want to control for your domain has a button or switch in the back end. The Admin Control Panel makes it far easier to navigate to key admin functions than any Microsoft server software. You can add, delete or suspend users, transfer ownership of all documents, create aliases, and change minimum password requirements.

2. Spend Staff Time On Training And Improvement, Not On Maintaining Systems

Properly maintaining an email and calendar server with 99.9% uptime is time-consuming and requires a skilled admin to be available nearly 24/7 to troubleshoot errors. Google Apps frees that time and delivers a plethora of additional tools. The most popular alternative to Google Apps in legal services has been Microsoft Exchange. The consensus is that any shop will have to dedicate a portion of tech just to maintain Exchange and anticipate problems. The time needed to just keep things running can now be used to train and support users.

3. Google Apps Is Free For Non-Profits

One of the major advantages of Google Apps is that it is very cheap. Most legal aid organizations will be able to use Google Apps for free since they have 501(c)(3) status and under 3,000 users (more on Google non-profit status eligibility). If you are not eligible as a non-profit, Google Apps is still relatively cheap, and you can find their full billing Info on their website.

This includes the following features:

- ❖ Gmail, Calendar, and other Google Services
- ❖ Email migration tools
- ❖ Extensibility APIs
- ❖ Customer Service

Compare this price to the cheapest options from Google Docs' competitors:

- ❖ WordPerfect Office: $179.99/seat (no non-profit discount)
- ❖ Microsoft Office: $199.99/seat ($30/seat with non-profit discount)
- ❖ Apple iWork: $79.00

These tools replicate only a tiny part of the Google Apps ecosystem - the word processor. Full enterprise systems such as Microsoft Exchange with Sharepoint add significant additional costs.

4. Google Apps' Unique Capabilities Can Help Legal Services Organizations

Beyond replacing functions provided by other software, Google Apps offer distinctive features meant to change and improve office functioning.

A. **Collaboration:** Features like document-sharing, simultaneous editing, shared calendars, and chat makes group work easier, and encourage office members to become more aware of each others' work.

B. **Searching:** Documents and emails in Google Apps are designed to be searched rather than sorted by the user. This means that users can spend less time organizing files, and don't have to know and remember a particular system of organization to find what they are looking for. As demonstrated by the LSNC Findability Project, moving to a system where nearly all office data is searchable through Google Search Appliance (GSA) can help offices significantly increase their effectiveness.

C.   **Integration:** Google Apps are designed to interact with each other, and are more powerful in combination.

Useful Google Apps You Probably Aren't Using

1. Measure

Need to get a quick measurement of a physical object in your home or office and don't have your trusty tape measure handy? (What you were thinking, heading to work without a measuring apparatus in your pocket?!) Well, fret no more: Google's Measure app is up to the task. Just fire up Measure, aim your phone's camera at any object around you a box you need to ship, a ship you need to box, or anything in between, and within a matter of seconds, the app will help you drag a virtual tool onto the image and get a real-world measurement of any of its sides. The measure can even handle metric units, if that's your jam, and can estimate elevation along with distance.

2. PhotoScan

Further blurring the lines between our physical and virtual worlds is PhotoScan, which lets you capture impressively high-quality and glare-free images from your phone's camera and then save 'em as digital files. PhotoScan directs you through the process of capturing multiple angles of a printed photo and then does all the dirty work of cropping it, straightening it, and just generally making it look good. It's like having a full-fledged scanner in your pocket only, far more practical to carry.

3. Files

Google's default Android file manager has gotten reasonably decent over the years, but you know what's weird? Google makes a much better and more capable version of the same basic thing. It's just up to you to find it. The aptly named Files app (which isn't the same as the Files app that comes preinstalled on certain Android phones) lets you browse through your phone's local storage in a clean and easy-to-use interface. It makes it super-simple to eliminate unneeded junk on your device and free up space, too, and it even has a built-in and fuss-free system for wirelessly sharing files with other Android phones in the area. Files aren't as fully featured as some of the more advanced third-party file manager apps, but it's pretty darn useful — and if your Android file management needs are relatively basic, it'll be more than enough to get the job done.

4. Trusted Contacts

This next Google Android app is one of those things that's so practical, you'll wonder why your phone hasn't always had it. Trusted Contacts lets you establish location-sharing relationships with your friends, family members, or anyone else you know and love (or maybe just kinda-sorta like). Once both people have installed the app and approved the relationship, either person can request the other's location at any time. If the recipient doesn't respond after five minutes, their last known location will automatically be sent. And it works even if their phone is off or out of range. Peace of mind has never been easier.

5. Voice Access

Android's long been exceptional at letting you control your phone by voice dating back to well before the big Google Assistant rebranding but with a little help from an out-of-the-way Google app, you can take your phone's hands-free potential to new heights. The app is a little somethin' called Voice Access. It's technically an Android accessibility feature, but it can be incredibly useful for just about anyone.

Plain and simple, Voice Access lets you control every single part of your phone-using experience simply by speaking. Once you fire up the system, you can tell your phone to go back (look, Ma, no awkward gestures!), go home, or adjust more or less any element of your phone's settings. You can ask it to long-press an item, scroll in any direction on an item, select or unselect text, and place your cursor anywhere you want. It can even handle text editing and let you get around apps and websites without lifting a finger via its clever on-screen numbering system. Whether you have a physical need for that sort of control or just think you'd benefit from the convenience, it's one heck of an option to have at your fingertips.

6. Google My Business

This next one's pretty specific, but if you're operating your own business or responsible for your company's online presence in any way Google's My Business app is worth snagging. The app gives you a single streamlined portal for controlling your company's presence within Google. You can respond to reviews, tweak your business's profile, and even get notifications whenever a customer (or potential customer) attempts to connect with you. For the smaller business owners among us, it could be invaluable.

7. Google Opinion Rewards

I've mentioned Opinion Rewards several times over the years, but it's still something most typical users remain woefully unaware of. If you're among those not yet using it, start now because it's just a way to get free Google Play Store credit for taking the occasional quick survey.

8. Google Arts & Culture

Hang onto this one for your next dull business-trip moment: Google Arts & Culture lets you explore national parks and monuments, zoom up close into famous works of art, and even take virtual tours of entire museums right from your mobile device. The app is just jam-packed with cool views of fascinating things from around the world, and it provides a welcome mental diversion no matter where you might physically be.

9. Wallpapers

This last selection is the app that controls wallpaper picking for Google's Pixel line of phones, but it's available broadly and if you don't have a Pixel device, you can think of it as an upgrade to your system's default wallpaper selection tool. The aptly named Wallpapers makes finding a background for your home screen a fun adventure, with options for selecting stunning static or motion-based images in a variety of different categories from landscapes, seascapes, and planets to art and geometric shapes.

The best part, though, is the way Wallpapers can automatically change your wallpaper to a new image every day within any category that floats your boat (including, if you're so inclined, your images). It makes for a nice little surprise when you're moving between your various Very Important Work Duties.

Chapter 2: Google Drive

What Is Google Drive?

Google Drive is a cloud-based storage solution that allows you to save files online and access them anywhere from any smartphone, tablet, or computer. We won't get too technical here, but Google Drive is Google's cloud storage solution. It allows you to store your media and documents on Google servers so you can free up space on your hard drive and access them from just about any device with an internet connection.

Before we dive into all the features and show you how to use Google Drive, let's talk about a few basic things you have to know. The first is that you need a Google account to use the service. It's free of charge and can be set up in a few minutes. The account gives you access to all of Google's services, including Drive, Gmail, Photos, YouTube, Play Store, and so on.

Using a cloud storage service like Google Drive has plenty of advantages, such as easier file sharing and having a remote location to backup your files. But when compared to competitors like DropBox and Apple's iCloud service, Google Drive's popularity is built on useful collaborative tools and built-in integrations with

Google's suite of products and services. If you have a Google account, you already have 15 GB of free storage on Google Drive. So how to take advantage of all that space? Our guide covers all the basics, from how to use Google Drive to upload and access files on any device, to all the tools that make collaboration with others a breeze.

How Does Google Drive Work?

Think of Google Drive as a latter-day hard drive. Google Drive gives you the power to upload and save a range of file types documents, photos, audio, and videos to Google servers, or the "cloud. Drive can serve as a backup solution, or as a way to free up space on your device.

To understand why Google Drive is so popular, it's important to note that it's built to work seamlessly with Google. And one of Drive's best features is its integration with Google's office suite of cloud-native apps, which, if you have experience with Microsoft Office, will look familiar. Most users will gravitate to these programs, which include Google Docs, Sheets, Slides, and more. Not only do they let you create and edit documents, but they're also equipped with intuitive tools that allow for real-time collaboration.

Here Is A Breakdown Of The Most Commonly Used Google Drive Applications:

Google Drive works with an integrated suite of apps powered by Google.

Some Of Google Drive's Other Key Features:

Storing Files: By default, Google gives you 15 GB of free storage space across Gmail, Google Drive, and Google Photos. If you ever hit that limit, you can always pay for more space by upgrading to a Google One account.

Sharing Files: Files are private until you share them. But at any time, you can invite others to view, edit, or download files and documents.

Accessing Files From Anywhere: Files can be accessed from any smartphone, tablet, or computer. Offline access is also available.

Comprehensive Search: Drive can recognize images and even text in scanned documents, making searching for files even easier.

Secure Storage: Drive files are protected by an AES256 or AES128 encryption, the same security protocol used on other Google services.

How To Use Google Drive
Access To Google Drive Requires A Google Account.

To get started with Google Drive, you'll need to make a Google account, if you don't already have one. Creating a Google account is free, and gives you access to Google Drive, as well as other Google Services, such as Gmail, Google Calendar, and Google Photos. Once you've signed up for an account (or signed into an existing account), you can access Google Drive in your browser by going to drive.google.com. This will bring you to Drive's web interface, which is fairly intuitive and easy to navigate. As you begin to familiarize yourself with all the things you can do with Google Drive, you'll most likely want to first learn how to upload, create, manage, and share files.

Uploading And Creating Files

To get started, you can drag and drop files into Drive, or create something new. To access files on Google Drive, you'll need to upload them. There are two ways you can upload files from the web client, and they're both straightforward. The first method is the simpler of the two, and it involves dragging the file or folder from your desktop and dropping it into the browser window. The second option is to click on the "New button on the top-left side of the screen and select either "File upload or "Folder upload." You can also use the "New button to create a new file, document, spreadsheet, or presentation. Depending on your needs, just click on the app from the dropdown menu. All new files are automatically saved and accessible from your Drive.

Managing And Organizing Files And Folders

Creating folders is an easy way to organize your files. Once you have enough files, you may want to organize them. Much like organizing files on your desktop, the easiest way to manage your Drive is to create folders. To create a new folder on the web interface, navigate to your Drive, and click "New, then "Folder." After you name your folder, you'll be able to drag and drop files to the folder, which can found under "My Drive the pane to the left of your screen. If you no longer need a file and want to keep your Drive tidy, the easiest way to delete a file is to right-click on the file. This will bring up a context menu. From there, select "Remove. Alternatively, you can select the file you want to delete and then click the trash icon on the upper-right hand corner of your screen.

Sharing Files And Folders

Sharing files is as easy as a right-click. The biggest draw of Google Drive is the ability to share files and folders with others. From sharing videos to entire Drive folders, Drive makes sharing simple. To share a Google Drive file or folder, right-click on it to bring up the context menu, then click "Share." From there, you'll be able to add collaborators using their email address and decide whether people can edit, comment on, or simply just view the file. Any files created in Drive have the option to be edited by multiple people at once, meaning you'll be able to collaborate with others in real-time.

Accessing Google Drive

Now that we have some basics out of the way, it's important to note that there are multiple ways to access your Drive. In addition to using Drive in your web browser, you can also access the cloud from your mobile device or desktop.

Google Drive On Mobile

The Google Drive mobile app allows you to access files anywhere. The Google Drive mobile app is available for both iOS and Android, and it's a must-have for anyone who wants immediate access to their files from anywhere. The app lets you view, download, upload, and delete files, all from your mobile device. If you're interested in creating, editing, and organizing files on-the-go, you'll need to download the relevant standalone mobile app. Each app has offline support built-in so they can function on their own without an internet connection, but they're also designed to work seamlessly with the Google Drive app:

- ❖ Google Docs for iOS or Android
- ❖ Google Sheets for iOS or Android
- ❖ Google Slides for iOS or Android
- ❖ Google Drive on desktop

Back-Up And Sync Allow You To Synchronize Local Files To Google Drive.

If you're more inclined to work on a desktop than in a web browser, Back-Up and Sync is an app for Mac and PC that makes it easy to back up files to Google Drive. The desktop client integrates seamlessly with Google Drive and simplifies the backup process. Not only does it require minimal effort to use, but it's also easy to install:

How To Install Back Up And Sync On Mac

Once installed, a new Google Drive folder will be created on your computer. Any files or folders moved into this folder are automatically uploaded to Google Drive, so you can access them anywhere and from any device.

Google Drive Tips And Tricks

Google Drive is rife with intuitive features and tools, and it takes regular use to uncover the best ones for your wants and needs. Here are a few tips first-time and power users should know.

Google Drive Gmail Integration

Gmail is an especially useful integration. If Gmail is your main email client, good news: It offers full integration with Google Drive. When composing a message, you can attach a Google Drive file by clicking the Google Drive icon found on the toolbar at the bottom of your screen. Conversely, Gmail makes it easy to save attachments to Drive. By positioning your mouse over the attachment, you'll have the option to either download the file or save it to Drive. Simply click the Google Drive icon and choose the folder.

Accessing Files Offline

To manage offline settings, access your settings page. Another useful tip is Drive allows you to view and edit files offline without connecting to the internet. While you can always download files or folders directly to your computer for offline access, offline mode lets you view and edit Google Docs, Google Sheets, and Google Slides, with any changes automatically synced when a connection is available again. To turn on offline mode, navigate to your Drive and click the gear icon at the top right-hand corner of your screen. Once in your settings, you'll be able to turn on offline mode by checking the box next to "Offline."

Converting Files To Google Drive Format

It's easy to convert a file to Google Drive format for easy collaboration. Google Drive supports many different file types, but if you plan on editing files in Google Drive, they will need to be converted to the Google Drive format. Doing so will allow you to easily share the file with others and unlock tools so you can collaborate with others in real-time. Files that can be converted to Google Drive format are:

- ❖ Text documents (.doc, .docx, .html, .txt, .rtf, .pdf)
- ❖ Spreadsheets (.xls, .xlsx, .ods, .csv)
- ❖ Presentations (.ppt, .pps, .pptx)

To convert a file to Google Drive format, simply right-click on the file, choose "Open With, and click the suggested app. For example, if you have a Microsoft Word document, you'll be able to convert it to a Google Doc document.

Google Drive Apps And Services

When it comes to how Google Drive works with apps and other Google services, there's a lot to explore. We already covered Drive's core office suite Docs, Sheets, and Slides which can be understood as replacements for Microsoft Word, Excel, and PowerPoint. While most users will be happy using these apps, Drive also supports and integrates with other Google services such as Google Jamboard.

Add-Ons

Add-ons allow you to do more with Google Docs, Sheets, Slides, and Forms. Google's suite of office programs are superb on their own, but you can make them more suitable to your needs with add-ons. There are many helpful add-ons to help you do more with Google Docs, Sheets, Slides, and Forms. To explore add-ons, just open or create any file, then navigate to "Add-onsin the toolbar at the top of your screen. Visit the Chrome web store to see what's available.

How To Use Google Drive With Third-Party Apps?

Drive is connected with Google's office productivity suite that includes Google Docs, Sheets, and Slides, which rival Microsoft's Word, Excel, and PowerPoint. Although these three services have their dedicated website, every document you create is automatically saved in Drive. Drive also supports other Google services like Google Forms, Google Drawings, and more.

You can create a document straight from Drive's web interface or the mobile app, which will then take you to the Google Doc's dedicated website. How exactly? Click the blue New button in the top-left corner of the website and then select Google Docs, Google Sheets, or Google Slides. On mobile, tap the blue + icon and select one of the three options mentioned in the previous sentence. No matter which option you choose, you'll always be able to access all created documents from your PC, mobile device, as well as the Drive folder on your computer. Google Drive also integrates with many third-party apps. These include:

- ❖ DocHub (signing PDFs),
- ❖ Pixlr Express (photo editor),
- ❖ Draw.io (diagrams), and many others.

One third-party app that works with Google Drive is WhatsApp, where you can store your older messages on the cloud service. In even better news, WhatsApp made a change that lets people store messages on Google Drive without having them count towards their storage limits. You can check out the full list via the web interface: click the New button and select More followed by Connect more apps. When you see something you like, click the Connect button to integrate it with Drive.

Third-Party App Integrations

In addition to add-ons, Drive is built to work seamlessly with hundreds of third-party applications that would allow split and merge PDFs, digitally sign documents, create diagrams, and more all from within Drive. For the productivity obsessed, you can also link Drive to several productivity tools for a more seamless workflow. Here's a small sample:

- ❖ Google Drive for Slack
- ❖ Google Drive for Evernote
- ❖ Google Drive for Asana
- ❖ Google Drive for AirTable
- ❖ Google Drive for Trello

How To Upload And Download Google Drive Files?

To access your files on Google Drive, you first need to upload them on the wcb, PC, or mobile client. First, we'll talk about the web client, where there are two ways to upload files to Drive.

The First Is The Drag And Drop Method: select a file you want to upload from your PC, drag it to Drive in a browser window and drop it. This works for both individual files as well as folders. The second option is to click on the New button located in the top-left corner of the website and either select File upload or Folder upload (image above). Then choose the files or folders you want to upload, click on Open or Upload, and you're good to go.

An even easier method of uploading to Google's cloud server is to take advantage of Google Drive for Desktop. Just drag the documents you want to upload and drop them into the Drive folder. It works the same as transferring files from one folder to another on your computer, although it may take a while for the files to sync.

Uploading files from your mobile device is equally easy. Open the Drive app, click the + icon in the bottom-right corner, and select the file you want to send to the cloud. You can also quickly upload files by opening them, tapping the Share button, then Save to Drive.

Downloading files from Google Drive is also fast and easy on any device with an internet connection. If you're using Google Drive for Desktop, anything you upload can be copied to any other folder on your computer just like any other file. You can also download files from the web client by right-clicking and clicking Download. This works for both individual files and entire folders.

On mobile devices, it can be more convenient to leave the files in the cloud and just open them when you need them, but there are some situations where you'll need to find that Google Drive download button. All you need to do is find your file in the app, tap the three dots on the right, then Download, and you're good to go.

How To Organize And Delete Files On Google Drive?

You can organize the files in Drive the same way you would on your PC. You can leave them all in one place (My Drive) or put them in different folders. To create a folder in the web client, click on the New button, and then select Folder. You can also right-click in the Drive folder on your computer and create a new folder like you normally would on Windows.

How To Create A New Folder In Google Drive

To move files into a folder on the web, simply use the drag and drop method for the web client and the Drive folder. This also works on mobile, but in my experience, it's faster if you tap the More actions icon (three vertical dots) next to a file, select the Move option, and then choose the new location for the file.

How To Delete Drive Files?

Since storage space is at a premium in the cloud, it's important to know how to delete Drive files to clear up space. The easiest option on the web is to select a file or folder and press the delete key on your keyboard. This works for both the web client and Drive folder. To delete a Drive document from your mobile device, tap the More actions icon next to the file (three vertical dots) and select Remove.

How To Use Google Drive Offline?

Having your files online is great for accessing them from multiple devices, but it can also mean you won't be able to see or edit them without an internet connection. Fortunately, this isn't the case with Google Drive. The service has an offline mode, allowing you to access files while you're not connected to the internet. You can view and edit files including Google Docs, Sheets, and Slides, with all the changes being synchronized automatically when an internet connection is established again.

You have to turn on offline access individually for each device. On your computer, open the settings menu, and enable the Offline mode (image above). Also, make sure to download the Google Docs offline Chrome extension. Once that's done, you can visit Drive's website to view or edit your files. But keep in mind that you have to use the Chrome browser for this to work. Of course, you can also open files via the Drive folder on your computer, which will then open up in Chrome.

Things are a bit different on mobile devices. You have to open the Drive app, tap the More actions icon (three vertical dots) next to a file, and then select Available offline. Alternatively, you can long-press on a file and then select additional ones and follow the same procedure to enable offline mode for multiple files at the same time.

Chapter 3: Google Doc

Google Docs is one of the most beloved word processing apps out there. It is a free, web-based, and lets you do everything a typical word processing app should: create documents, edit text, add pictures, and more. Google Docs is perhaps one of the world's best data-driven ingenious products that provide solutions to data security, team collaboration, integration, and an easier approach to document storage amongst others. Vice-grip or not, Google sure has created numerous products and services to help everyone, whether it's for personal or business use.

Each Google product; Drive, Keep, Docs, Sheets, Photos, Calendar, Gmail, etc - has a streamlined interface fitted with features that boast of high-end intelligence and security (it's Google, you shouldn't expect less).

However, what makes it stand out is how it helps teams collaborate, you can share documents with anyone, others can add comments, you can chat inside docs, and a lot more. More so, it also has a huge library of 3rd-party add-ons.

What Is Google Docs?

Google Docs is a word processor included as part of a free, web-based software office suite offered by Google within its Google Drive service. This service also includes Google Sheets and Google Slides, a spreadsheet, and a presentation program respectively. Google Docs is available as a web application, mobile app for Android, iOS, Windows, BlackBerry, and as a desktop application on Google's ChromeOS. The app is compatible with Microsoft Office file formats. The application allows users to create and edit files online while collaborating with other users in real-time. Edits are tracked by the user with a revision history presenting changes. An editor's position is highlighted with an editor-specific color and cursor. A permissions system regulates what users can do. Updates have introduced features using machine learning, including "Explore", offering search results based on the contents of a document, and "Action items", allowing users to assign tasks to other users.

Google Docs

Just like learning any other mastery, let's start with a basic understanding of how to get around Google Docs.

1. Creating, Naming, Saving Docs

To create a Google document, simply click on the + on your Google Docs homepage. When you create a document, it will be named as Untitled Document by default, to rename, simply:

- ❖ Click the name at the top of the file
- ❖ Type a new name
- ❖ Press Enter

Since Google Docs have an Auto-save feature, avoid the stress and effort of manually saving your work.

2. Formatting Text

Using the Google Docs toolbar, you can change the text, the font style, and even assign specific font style for particular sections of the text. Along with this, Google Docs provides editing options like paragraph spacing and alignment.

3. Creating A Table Of Contents

On your, Google Docs click where you want the table of contents to be placed. Click Insert on the menu bar and select Table of contents. You can choose With page numbers or With blue links. In case you want to delete the table, right-click and select Delete.

4. Inserting Images And Tables

Choose Image from the Insert tab and select the following option – Upload, Take a snapshot, By URL, Your albums, Google Drive and

Search. Make sure that the image you select must be less than 50 MB and should be one of the following file formats – .gif, .jpg, or .png.

5. Translating Docs

Select Tools from the menu bar and choose translate document. Enter a name for the newly translated document and select a language of your choice, a translated copy of your document will open in a new window.

If the language you selected has non-Latin characters, either type the phonetic spelling of a word in Latin characters, then click the best match from the options or draw characters in a panel in the bottom right of the screen and click the best match from the options. These are often used to translate documents for languages like Hindi and Mandarin.

6. Publishing Docs On The Web

On your Google Doc's menu bar, click File, and select Publish to the web. The entire document will be published on the internet, however, files containing spreadsheets or presentation formats might have more publishing requirements. Share the file by sending it in the URL or embed it on your website.

After selecting the option, publish to the web, a window will open, click Embed. Select Publish and copy the code in the text box and paste it into your site or blog. After the basic crash course, let's get down to the nitty-gritty of things. Google Docs like other G Suite applications comes with a hefty number of impressive features that help in boosting the overall productivity of businesses and individuals.

How To Create A Public Google Docs Templates

Step 1: Create a document in Google Docs that you'd like to use as a template and you can add further modification of your own as well.

Step 2: Open Google Docs Templates and click Submit a template.

Step 3: Click Choose from your Google Docs

Step 4: Select the template you had created in step 1.

Step 5: Type in a description for the template and make sure it's at least a sentence otherwise Google might reject the template.

Step 6: A drop-down list of Categories will be shown, choose the option which seems apt. If it's a project meeting template, you can choose the category Business or if it's a template for a legal contract, categorize the template under Legal.

Step 7: Select the language the template was originally written in.

Step 8: Click the Submit template.

Step 9: Go to your template gallery page and select your custom made template and start working.

How To Create A Private Google Docs Template

Step 1: After creating your template document.

Step 2: Go to your Google Drive and right-click File.

Step 3: Select Make a Copy.

Step 4: Use a copy of the original template document privately.

How To Convert A PDF To Google Doc Format

If you have PDF documents that you'd prefer to have in text format on your Google Drive account, being able to convert PDFs to Google Doc will allow you to do that. However, PDF conversion isn't as straightforward as many people think. Sure, it's easy to quickly convert a PDF file to a Google Doc file. However, what you enjoy in convenience comes at a price in formatting and style.

Thankfully there are workarounds to keep original formatting from the PDF document. Whether you opt for this approach depends on whether you care much about the formatting in the first place.

Preparing To Convert A PDF To Google Doc Format

Before you convert a PDF file over to Google Doc format, you want to make sure that all of the information that's supposed to be part of the PDF document is all in place.

For example, if you're converting a PDF lease agreement, the agreement should be filled out with all of the relevant information first. You can do this with anyone of your favorite PDF editors. If you don't have a PDF editor on your computer, the easiest way to do this is by using a free online PDF editing tool like Smallpdf.

Quickly Convert A PDF To Google Doc Format

❖ The fastest method to convert any PDF file straight into Google Doc format is to initiate the conversion process from right inside Google Drive.

❖ Upload the PDF file into your Google Drive account by right-clicking inside any folder and selecting Upload Files.

❖ Once the PDF is uploaded to Google Drive, you can right-click the file and select Open With, then select Google Docs.

❖ Google Docs will automatically convert the PDF document into Google Docs format.

❖ What you'll notice immediately is that while the text all imports correctly from most PDF documents, the formatting is rarely perfect.

Common Mistakes That Occur During Automatic Conversion Include:

❖ Double spacing becomes single spaced
❖ Simple spacing reverts to no space
❖ Indentation is removed

- ❖ Numbered or bullet lists become one paragraph
- ❖ Fields in fillable forms are removed
- ❖ If you made sure to fill out the fields in the PDF document before the conversion, the text in those fields will convert over fine.

However, this automatic conversion approach is best used if you don't really care about formatting and just want to transfer all of the text from a PDF document into a Google Doc.

Convert A PDF To Google Doc Format With Formatting

There is a way to get around this formatting failure, and that's taking advantage of Microsoft Word's more accurate conversion process. If you use Microsoft Word to convert PDF to a Microsoft Word document, you can then convert that document to a Google Doc document. All of the original formattings will be retained and brought over.

To do this, open Microsoft Word on your computer.

From inside Word, select Open from the main menu and browse to the PDF file you want to convert. You'll see a pop-up window notifying you that the file needs to be converted from PDF format. Select OK to continue. When the conversion is finished, you'll see the document open in Word. Word does an excellent job keeping the original formatting in place. Unlike Google Docs, this typically includes spacing, indentations, bold, and more.

You may need to select Enable Editing at the top of the window to save the file to your PC in Word format.

Select File, Save As, and save the Word document to your PC. The file will save with a docx extension.

Open your Google Drive account and navigate to the folder where you want to store the converted PDF file. Right-click inside the folder and select Upload files. Navigate to the docx file you saved and select Open.

This will bring the document into Google Drive as a Word file. Right-click the file, select Open With, and select Google Docs. This will convert the Word document into Google Docs format. As you can see, this newly converted file contains a much better-formatted version of the original PDF document.

To Complete The Conversion, Select File, And Save As Google Docs.

This will remove ".DOCX" at the top of the document and store the document as a full Google Doc. This approach may require a few extra steps, but if the formatting of the original PDF document is important to you, this is a good method to bring that formatting over.

Other Ways To Convert PDF Documents

There are plenty of other tools and approaches you can use to convert a PDF document to Word or Google Docs. The option you choose depends on which tools you have at your disposal.

- ❖ Use online or desktop PDF converter tools to convert from PDF to Word and then repeat the process above to convert the Word document to Google Docs.
- ❖ Use online tools to convert the PDF document to a JPG file and insert the JPG into your Google Doc.
- ❖ Use online tools to extract text out of the PDF document and insert the text into your Google Doc (if formatting doesn't matter at all).
- ❖ Use online OCR services to convert troublesome PDF files that don't convert easily into text format.

As you can see, when you want to convert PDFs to Google Docs, you have lots of great options available.

Tips On Sharing Files And Folders With Google Drive

The ability to share documents and work collaboratively is one of the most useful things about Google Drive! Here are some tips on how to get started.

Share a single item with specific people

Use this method when you know the email address (Hampshire or otherwise) of everyone with whom you are sharing.

Open a file in Google Docs, Sheets, or Slides.

In the top right corner, click Share.

Under "People" in the "Share with others" box, type the email address (Hampshire, or otherwise) of the person or Google Group you want to share with. Tip: Search for Hampshire contacts by typing a name in the box.

To choose if a person can view, comment, or edit the file, click the Down arrow next to the text box down arrow icon.

Click Done. The people you shared with will get an email letting them know you've shared a file.

Share A Single Item Using a Link

Use this method when you don't know everyone's email address, aren't sure if they all have a Google account, or simply want a document to be more widely available. You can have the link only available to the Hampshire community, or the whole world.

- ❖ Open a file in Google Docs, Sheets, or Slides.
- ❖ In the top right corner, click Share.
- ❖ Click "Get shareable link" in the top right of the "Share with others" box.

❖ To choose whether a person can view, comment, or edit the file, click the Down arrow next to "Anyone with the link." down arrow icon.

Note that the link will default to be viewable by Cornerstone College accounts only! To expand access to outside of Cornerstone, click the Down arrow next to "Anyone at Cornerstone College" and select "More" for additional options.

A file link will be copied to your clipboard. Paste the link in an email or anywhere you want to share it.

Sharing A Folder

If you plan to collaborate with a group of people regularly, such as within a department or for a class, we strongly suggest creating a shared folder or a shared drive (see below). Then every item placed in this folder will automatically be shared with the group.

Create A Folder

Go to drive.Cornerstone.edu

On the left, click New > Folder.

Enter a name for the folder.

Click Create.

Then, share the folder:

Select the name of the folder in Google Drive. At the top, click Share Share. Tip: You can also right-click the folder and choose Share.

Under "People" in the "Share with others" box, type the email address of the person or Google Group with whom you want to share. Tip: Search for contacts by typing a name in the box.

Make sure their access level is set to "Can Edit."

Shared Drives

Shared drives are shared spaces where teams can easily store, search, and access their files anywhere, from any device. Unlike files in My Drive, files in a shared drive belong to the team instead of an individual. Even if members leave, the files stay exactly where they are so your team can continue to share information and get work done.

Not Sure Whether To Use My Drive Or A Shared Drive?

Ask yourself these questions:

- ❖ Are the files of interest to most or all members of a particular project team?

- ❖ Do the files share a consistent theme?

If you answered "yes" to both questions, creating a new shared drive is a good idea. If the files are for a variety of projects, create multiple shared drives. For a comparison of My Drive and shared drives, see Differences between My Drive and shared drives.

View What Can You Do With Shared Drives? To Get Started

Changing the ownership of a file or folder. You may want to assign someone else to be the "owner" of a file or folder. The owner has full control over access, visibility, and can choose to delete the file.

How To Change Owners

- ❖ You can change who owns a file or folder in Drive.
- ❖ Go to Drive or Docs, Sheets, or Slides home screen.

Open The Sharing Box:

In Drive: Select the file or folder and click the share icon at the top share icon.

In A Docs, Sheets, Or Slides Home Screen: Open the file and click Share in the top-right corner of the file

If the new owner already has edit access, skip to Step 4. Otherwise, follow these steps:

- ❖ Type the email address of the new owner in the "Invite people" field
- ❖ Click Share and save.

- ❖ Click Advanced in the bottom-right corner of the sharing box.
- ❖ Click the drop-down menu next to the name of the person you want to own the file or folder.
- ❖ Select Is the owner.
- ❖ Click Done.

Google Docs Tips And Tricks

Google Docs Hacks

Discover the Google Docs feature that makes writing, editing, and sharing easier. Let's dive into the Google hacks that will save time and create efficiencies all around.

Fast Track Editing

We've all been there. You've taken the time to draft an impressive blog, white paper, or whatever else you've poured your heart in to. Now you're at the finish line, and it's time to tidy things up but you're running out of steam. The following tips call on Google to step in and lend you a hand.

Organize Your Document With An Outline

As you write your material, create sections using the Style drop-down as you go. Once complete, go to Tool and select "Document Outline." Google will automatically generate a table of content. Look to the left of your doc. You've not got an outline based on the headers you've applied. This is essential when you are working through a large document. Now you can click through sections with ease.

Perform Advanced Edits Via Spoken Command

Dictation can mean some real swift editing. Lucky for us, Google's voice command system supports a huge range of functions. Ask for specific phrases, words, paragraphs. You name it. With your voice alone, you can apply different formatting types to the text, cut, copy, paste, and even scroll through the documents or jump to parts of a page, all without lifting a finger. To become a pro at editing the lazy way, check out Google's guide to all possible voice commands.

Enrich Your Work

If you're struggling for inspiration, and your work is feeling a bit flat, listen up. These tips are designed to enrich your creations in Docs. Take inspiration from Google or your notes.

Call On Google To Clarify Definitions

For any content publishers reading, it's worth hammering home again how convenient the explore feature is. All you have to do is highlight the text you're pondering over, right-click for more options and hit explore to rack Google's brain (Google search).

You'll soon get to the bottom of anything and everything within Googles' extensive grasp. The Explore button can also be found on the bottom right-hand corner of your doc. It's the icon of a star inside a small speech bubble.

This feature provides instant suggestions based on the content in your document, including related topics to learn about, images to insert, or more content to check out in Docs. You can also find a related document from Drive or search Google right within Explore.

View Keep Notes While Working In Google Docs

To access your Keep notes, head to the Google Doc Tools menu. You should see an entry for Keep Notepad. The first time you open this, you will be prompted to enable the feature. Click on "TRY IT" to log in, and the Keep notepad will open as a sidebar in your document. If you're already using keep, you'll notice all of your notes arranged linearly. Scroll through the notes to find what you need. Note that the addition of Google Keep only works in Docs, it won't cross over to Sheets.

Collaboration In Google Docs

For a project that involves more than one pair of eyes, you need to learn to collaborate. With the following. Did you know that you can add up to fifty users per collaboration, and everyone can view and edit at the same time? While this might sound overwhelming, there's a trick or two to organize people's suggestions.

Go Into Suggestion Mode

In Suggestions mode, anyone with permission to edit a document can suggest edits to the document owner (instead of simply making changes). The document owner has a chance to review the suggestions and accept or reject each edit and keep track of who changed what. As you make changes to a document in Suggestions mode, everything you type becomes bracketed, and anything you delete gets a strike-through.

Suggestions mode is only available for Google Docs. To turn it on follow these instructions.

First, you need to enable tracked edits. To do this, click the pencil icon on the right-hand side of the toolbar and select 'Suggestions'. Now, when you type, or make changes, they appear with color-coded highlighting visible to anyone viewing the document. what you've added are visible in the document.

Click Tools, then Review Suggested Edits. A 'Suggesting' box will appear in the top right-hand corner of your document. Now, when you add any new text or delete any existing text.

When it is time to review the document, click on a suggested edit to activate its bubble in the right column. To accept an edit, click the checkmark to accept, to reject a suggestion, click the 'X'. If you're unsure about a suggestion, it's possible to leave a comment for the editor. Just reply within the edit bubble.

When there are many suggestions on a document, it can be difficult to follow the flow of the text. To preview what your text will look like with or without suggested edits, click 'Viewing' mode.

Google Doc Features To Boost Your Productivity

Who doesn't want to save time in the working day? Dismiss these productivity boosts tips at your peril.

Use Templates To Save Time

Yes, we covered the benefits of using templates earlier. How about templates specific for Google Docs. These are handy for recurring projects such as customer invoices and meeting proposals to save you starting from scratch each time. Find templates for everything from project proposals, onboarding notes, job-offer letters you can modify to your needs. More templates for things like statements of work and sales of work are available as add-ons.

Google Docs – Shortcut Keys

While some are toying with the idea of typing with their voice, others are just plain old school and can't imagine typing ideas into their Google document without a keyboard. Since you are at the keyboard typing voraciously, saving a considerable amount of time by using keyboard shortcuts might be a good option to consider. On your menu bar, go to Help > Keyboard shortcuts.

Different Platforms: Windows and Mac, have mostly common shortcut keys, like the ones illustrated in the table:

However, There Are Some Actions Which Have Distinct Shortcut Keys:

- ❖ If you are accessing Mozilla Firefox from a Mac enabled device, then use Ctrl + ~ to Search Menu
- ❖ To access Table menu on Google Chrome: Alt + B, other browsers: Alt + Shift + B
- ❖ Alt + I (in Google Chrome) or Alt + Shift + I (in other browsers) = Open the Insert menu.
- ❖ In Google Chrome: Alt + O, other browsers: Alt + Shift + O
- ❖ Accessibility menu (present when screen reader support is enabled), in Google Chrome: Alt + A, other browsers: Alt + Shift + A

Work Offline With Google Docs

Many users, even the die-hard fans of Google consider the biggest flaw for a cloud-based platform like Google Docs – the necessity of an internet connection. It makes you think – is keeping your work on Google Docs a smart option? Well, think again! A few quick steps and you can manage your entire workflow on Google Docs without an internet connection:

1. Enable Offline Settings

- ❖ Step 1: on your Google Docs Homepage, click
- ❖ Menu> Settings> Offline.
- ❖ Step 2: Switch on the offline sync capability.
- ❖ Step 3: A dialogue box opens up, Which requests permission to activate Google Docs offline – click the Enable Offline button.
- ❖ Step 4: Google will also notice that an extension is also required to be installed, click the Add Extension to complete the process.

2. Editing Offline

Once you have synced your Google document to offline mode, then it's the same procedure for editing as it is in the online mode. Though, there are some minor differences:

- ❖ Some features which will be deactivated like – Add-ons, Explore, Help (Except Keyboard Shortcuts)

- ❖ Next to the document name, at the top left of the screen, a small gray offline icon will appear.

3. New Documents

You can create new documents the usual way through Google Drive. Go to your Google Drive homepage: New>Google Docs.

4. Auto-Sync Offline Documents

All the documents and edits are stored in the local server, the next time you switch to online mode, Google Docs will automatically sync the changes made to offline files to the cloud.

Chapter 4: Google Sheets

This Google Sheets tutorial will help take you from an absolute beginner, or basic user, through to a confident, competent, intermediate-level user. Google Sheets is a hugely powerful tool, for everything from digital marketing to financial modeling, from project management to statistical analysis, in fact, just about any activity involving the recording and analysis of data.

And if you're (relatively) new, it pays dividends to learn how to use Google Sheets correctly. This tutorial will help you transition from newbie to ninja in short order!. If you're new to Google Sheets, then I recommend you start from the beginning of this article.

What Are Google Sheets?

Google Sheets is a free, cloud-based spreadsheet application. That means you open it in your browser window like a regular webpage, but you have all the functionality of a full spreadsheet application for doing powerful data analysis. It is the best of both worlds. Google Sheets is a spreadsheet app on steroids. It looks and functions much like any other spreadsheet tool but because it's an online app, it offers much more than most spreadsheet tools. Here are some of the things that make it so much better:

- ❖ It's a web-based spreadsheet that you can use anywhere no more forgetting your spreadsheet files at home.
- ❖ It works from any device, with mobile apps for iOS and Android along with its web-based core app.
- ❖ Google Sheets is free, and it's bundled with Google Drive, Docs, and Slides to share files, documents, and presentations online.
- ❖ It includes almost all of the same spreadsheet functions—if you know how to use Excel, you'll feel at home in Google Sheets.
- ❖ You can download add-ons, create your own, and write custom code.
- ❖ It's online, so you can gather data with your spreadsheet automatically and do almost anything you want, even when your spreadsheet isn't open.

Getting Started With Google Sheets

The best way to learn a tool like Sheets is to dive straight in. In this chapter, you'll learn how to:

- ❖ Create a Spreadsheet and Fill It With Data
- ❖ Format Data for Easy Viewing
- ❖ Add, Average, and Filter Data with Formulas
- ❖ Share, Protect, and Move Your Data

Why Use Google Sheets?

How's this for starters:

- ❖ It's free!
- ❖ It's collaborative, so teams can all see and work with the same spreadsheet in real-time.
- ❖ It has enough features to do complex analysis, but.
- ❖ it's also really easy to use.

How Is It Different From Excel?

No doubt you've heard of Microsoft Excel, the long-established heavyweight of the spreadsheet world. It's an incredibly powerful, versatile piece of software, used by approximately 750 million – 1 billion people worldwide. So yeah, a tough act to follow.

Google Sheets is similar in many ways, but also distinctly different in other areas. It has (mostly) the same set of functions and tools for working with data. Some people mistakenly call it "Google Excel" or "Google spreadsheets."

With The Risk Of Getting Into An Opinionated Debate About The Strengths/Weaknesses Of Each Platform, Here A Few Key Differences:

Google Sheets is cloud-based whereas Excel is a desktop program. With Sheets, you'll no longer have versions of your work floating around. Everyone always sees the same, most up-to-date version of Sheets, showing the same spreadsheet data.

- Collaboration is baked into Sheets, so it works extremely well. Excel is still trying to play catch up here.
- Both have charting tools and Pivot Table tools for data analysis, although Excel's are more powerful in both cases.
- Excel can handle much bigger datasets than Sheets, which has a limit of 2 million cells.
- Being a cloud-based program, Google Sheets integrates well with other online Google services and third-party sites.
- Both have scripting languages to extend their functionality and build custom tools. Google Sheets uses Apps Script (a variant of Javascript) and Excel uses VBA.

The Benefits Of Using Google Sheets For Marketing

First things first: Let's talk about the benefits of using Google Sheets for marketing purposes before we discuss more traditional options (like a standard Excel spreadsheet).

It's cloud-based: Cloud-based spreadsheets are automatically saved, stored, and maintained via a remote server. That means that you can access it online from anywhere, any time. Plus: Google Sheets is also available offline.

1. **It's Free:** No expensive software is required. Google Sheets is always 100% free.

2. It Works Across Devices: Modern marketers switch between devices throughout the day and Google Sheets accommodates that behavior. You can access and edit Google Sheet data from a wide variety of devices (like your smartphone, tablet, and computer).

3. Add-Ons Are Available: We'll get into the specifics of add-ons for Google Sheets a bit later, but the increased functionality and flexibility of these additional features make this spreadsheet tool even more versatile and powerful.

4. You Might Be Wondering: What's the difference between Google Sheets and Excel? The short answer is a price, collaboration, and flexibility.

While Excel requires a software subscription (which costs about $130), Google Sheets is free for all Google account holders. In terms of collaboration, Excel requires you to save and send a new version when edits are made, while Google Sheets automatically updates a single shared file for all team members. And lastly, because Google Sheets can accommodate many different integrations, it's often more flexible than a standalone software solution like Excel.

Common Google Sheets Terms To Know

Next, let's get familiar with some of the language and common terms used when referencing data within Google Sheets.

❖ **Column:** Columns are vertical cell sets.

- ❖ **Row:** Rows are horizontal cell sets.
- ❖ **Cell:** Cells are the single data points within a Google Sheet.
- ❖ **Range:** Range refers to a selection of cells across a column, row, or both.
- ❖ **Function:** Function refers to built-in operations for the Google Sheet that can be used to quickly calculate values, to manipulate data, and more.
- ❖ **Formula:** Formulas combine functions, rows, cells, columns, and ranges to generate a particular result.
- ❖ **Worksheet (Sheet):** The named sets of rows and columns making up your spreadsheet; one spreadsheet can have multiple sheets
- ❖ **Spreadsheet:** The entire document containing your worksheets

Understanding The Google Sheets Toolbar

One of the very first things to do is master the icons located in the Google Sheets toolbar. Doing so will help ensure you're getting the most out of its abilities and that you're saving time with shortcuts. Take a look at the screenshot below to identify some of the basic icons and their purposes within the toolbar.

How To Create A New Spreadsheet

When you're ready to create a new spreadsheet, you'll just need to follow a few quick steps to get started. Open Google Sheets and click

"File" > "New" > "Spreadsheet". Once you create your new spreadsheet, you can start adding data. If you want to work with an existing spreadsheet from Excel instead, you'll need to import that data into your new Google Sheet.

How To Convert Excel To Google Sheets

When you need to import an Excel spreadsheet into Google Sheets, go to "File" > "Import" > "Upload" and then select a file that's in one of the non-password protected formats (such as .xls, .csv, or .txt for example).

Sharing And Protecting Your Data

Once your Google Sheet is set up and populated, you'll want to think about how to share and protect your data. Data is automatically saved, so you don't need to worry about that part. You can select who you share your file with and whether they have edit, comment, or view permissions. You can also protect specific data within your sheet so that those who have access can only edit certain cells.

To Share A File:

❖ Go to "File" > "Share" (or just click the blue Share button in the top right corner)
❖ Enter the email address of who you'll be sharing the spreadsheet with
❖ Assign permission levels (such as "View only" or "Can edit")

- ❖ Click "Advanced" and select any additional privacy conditions needed

To Protect Data:

- ❖ Navigate to "Data" > "Protected Sheets and Ranges"
- ❖ Choose "Range" or "Sheet" (to protect an entire sheet)
- ❖ Select the data you'd like to protect
- ❖ Click "Set Permissions"
- ❖ Choose to show an error warning to anyone who attempts to edit or customize editing permissions for certain people.

Organizing Data In Google Sheets

Google Sheets is a powerful tool that can hold a ton of data. That means the more data you have, the harder it becomes to find it — that's when filtering comes in handy. Google Sheets has several filters that allow you to select the data you want to see and hide what you don't.

How To Hide Data

Google allows you to hide entire rows or columns. This becomes useful when you want to restrict views for sharing, or when you'd like to control the amount of data you're viewing at any given time. To hide a column, right-click the column you want to hide, then select "Hide Column". When you hide a column, two arrows will appear on the previous and subsequent columns. Click these to restore the column to full view.

How Do I Unhide Columns In Google Sheets?

To unhide a column in Google Sheets, simply look for the arrow icons that appear in the column's header bar. When you hover over one of the arrows, a white box framing the arrow will appear. Click either arrow to reveal the column.

How To Freeze Rows And Columns

Freezing will create a floating row or column as you scroll and keeps the data in those fields within your line of sight. For example, if you use the first row to label your columns, you can freeze that row so you don't have to remember what each column is as you scroll.

To freeze a row, select "View" > "Freeze" > "1 row" (or up to X rows).

How To Setup And Use Google Sheets Offline

If you need to use Google Sheets offline, just follow the steps outlined here to turn on offline access to your spreadsheets.

Keep In Mind:

- ❖ You must be connected to the internet.
- ❖ You'll need to use the Google Chrome browser (don't use incognito mode)

❖ You'll need to install and enable the Google Docs Offline Chrome extension.

Make sure you have enough free space on your device to save all your files.

From There:

❖ Open Chrome and make sure you're signed in.
❖ Go to drive.google.com/drive/settings.
❖ Check the box next to "Sync Google Docs, Sheets, Slides & Drawings files to this computer so that you can edit offline."
❖ To work on files offline from a computer, learn how to install Backup and Sync.

Google Sheets Functions & Skills You Should Know

How To Create A Pivot Table

Select the cells with source data you want to use in your pivot table. Note: Each column will need a header.

In the menu at the top, click "Data" > "Pivot table." Click the pivot table sheet (if it's not already open).

In the side panel, next to "Rows" or "Columns," click "Add" and then choose a value. Note: Sometimes you will see recommended pivot tables based on the data you've selected. To add a pivot table, under "Suggested," select a pivot table.

In the side panel, next to "Values," click "Add", then choose the value you want to see over your rows or columns. You can change how your data is listed, sorted, summarized, or filtered.

Next to what you want to change, click the down arrow.

How To Remove Duplicates

- ❖ Select the cell in which you'd like to remove the duplicated info.
- ❖ Enter the function =UNIQUE
- ❖ Select the cells you would like to pull data from
- ❖ Close the parentheses. Your function should look something like this: =UNIQUE(A: A)

How To Create A Drop-Down List

Next to "Criteria," choose an option:

Click "Data" > "Data validation".

Select the cell or cells in which you want to create a drop-down list. List from a range: Choose the cells that will be included in the list.

List of items: Enter items, separated by commas and no spaces.

The cells will have a down arrow. To remove the arrow, uncheck the "Display in-cell button to show list".

If you enter data in a cell that doesn't match an item on the list, you'll see a warning. If you want people to only enter items from the list, choose "Reject input" next to "On invalid data".

Click "Save". The cells will show a drop-down list. To change the color of a cell-based on the option, use conditional formatting (refer to the section above).

How To Make A Graph

❖ Select the cells you want to include in your chart. To label your chart, add a header row or column.

❖ Click "Insert" > "Chart".

❖ In the side panel, click "Data" > under "Chart type," choose a chart.

❖ To edit your chart, click "Customize."

Google Sheets Cheat Sheet

1. Customize Your Spreadsheet And Data.

Note: To improve compatibility with Microsoft Excel keyboard shortcuts, you can override browser shortcuts

2. Work With Rows, Columns, And Cells.

Add Rows, Columns, And Cells: Select the row, column, or cell near where you want to add your new entry. Right-click the highlighted row, column, or cell and then insert and then choose where to insert the new entry.

Delete, Clear, Or Hide Rows And Columns: Right-click the row number or column letter and then delete, Clear, or Hide.

Delete Cells: Select the cells and right-click and then delete cells and then shift left or Shift up.

Move Rows Or Columns: Select the row number or column letter and drag it to a new location.

Move Cells:

- ❖ Select the cells.
- ❖ Point your cursor to the top of the selected cells until a hand appears.
- ❖ Drag the cells to a new location.

Freeze Header Rows And Columns: Keep a row or column in the same place as you scroll through your spreadsheet. On the menu bar, click View and then freeze and choose an option.

3. Click Share to share your spreadsheet and then choose what collaborators can do. They'll also receive an email notification.

4. Collaborate with your team in real-time.

5. Create different versions and copies of your spreadsheet.

- ❖ **Make A Copy:** Create a duplicate of your spreadsheet. This is a great way to create templates.
- ❖ **Download As:**Download your spreadsheet in other formats, such as Excel or PDF.
- ❖ **Email As An Attachment:** Email a copy of your spreadsheet.
- ❖ **Version History:** See all the changes you and others have made to the spreadsheet or revert to earlier versions.
- ❖ **Publish To The Web:** Publish a copy of your spreadsheet as a webpage or embed your spreadsheet on a website.

6. Work With Functions.

Your most important Excel functions exist in Sheets, too. Here are a few of the things you can do.

AVERAGE: Statistical   Returns the numerical average value in a dataset, ignoring the text.

AVERAGEIFS: Statistical   Returns the average of a range that depends upon multiple criteria.

CHOOSE: Lookup Returns an element from a list of choices based on an index.

COUNT: Statistical   Returns the count of the number of numeric values in a dataset.

COUNTIF: Statistical Returns a conditional count across a range.

DATE: Date Converts a provided year, month, and day into a date.

FIND: Text Returns the position at which a string is first found within the text.

GETPIVOTDATA: Text Extracts an aggregated value from a pivot table that corresponds to the specified row and column headings.

IF: Logical Returns one value if a logical expression is true and another if it is false.

INDEX: Lookup Returns the content of a cell, specified by row and column offset.

INT: Math Rounds a number down to the nearest integer that's less than or equal to it.

LOOKUP: Lookup Looks through a row or column for a key and returns the value of the cell is a result range located in the same position as the search row or column.

MATCH: Lookup Returns the relative position of an item in a range that matches a specified value.

MAX: Statistical Returns the maximum value in a numeric dataset.

MIN: Statistical Returns the minimum value in a numeric dataset.

NOW: Date Returns the current date and time as a date value.

ROUND: Math Rounds a number to a certain number of decimal places according to standard rules.

SUM: Math Returns the sum of a series of numbers and/or cells.

SUMIF: Math Returns a conditional sum across a range.

TODAY: Date Returns the current date as a date value.

VLOOKUP: Lookup Searches down the first column of a range for a key and returns the value of a specified cell in the row found.

Chapter 5: Google Slides

Google Slides is a presentation program included as part of a free, web-based software office suite offered by Google within its Google Drive service. The service also includes Google Docs and Google Sheets, a word processor and spreadsheet respectively. Google Slides is available as a web application, mobile app for Android, iOS, Windows, BlackBerry, and as a desktop application on Google's ChromeOS. The app is compatible with Microsoft PowerPoint file formats.

Slides allow users to create and edit presentations online while collaborating with other users in real-time. Edits are tracked by the user with a revision history that tracks changes to the presentation. Each editor's position is highlighted with an editor-specific color/cursor and the system regulates what users can do through varying degrees of permissions. Updates have introduced features using machine learning, including "Explore", offering suggested layouts and images for presentations, and "Action items", allowing users to assign tasks to other users.

Is Google Slides Free?

Yes. Google Slides is free to use (along with other G Suite offerings such as Docs, Drive, Sheets, and more) as long as you have a Google account – which is also free. This includes web, mobile, and desktop apps. Whilst companies using G Suite can upgrade to a paid version with more business functionality, for the individual user the free version offers all the tools they're likely to need.

What Is Google Slides?

Maybe you've been hearing about Google Slides, but you aren't sure how it differs. What is Google Slides used for, and how does it differ from other apps?

There are many differences between Google Slides and traditional presentation apps. Here are three key principles to keep in mind when you're learning Google Slides:

It's Still Relatively New: PowerPoint was built in the '90s. Google Slides is a browser-first experience that set the tone for how powerful apps that live inside your web browser can be.

It's Connected: Because Google Slides is a browser-based app, it hooks into other web-connected services. That means collaboration and connecting to other apps is easy.

It's Simplified: Google is a company that focuses on simplifying the user experience. It's easy to use any of their apps so that tasks like learning how to use Google Slides is easy.

If you want to learn more about how to use Google Slides, we've got a guide that's right for you. It helps you learn how to access Google Slides and provides a complete Google Slides guide for beginners:

How To Access Google Slides

Google Slides is part of Google Drive which you can access in several ways:

From Gmail: If you are already in Gmail, you can click the "Drive" link in the black toolbar at the top.

Web Address: Or you can just type in the direct address: https://drive.google.com

How To Create A New Presentation

Once you are in Google Drive you can create a new presentation as follows:

- ❖ Click the red "Create" button in the top left corner
- ❖ Then click "Presentation" from the drop-down menu
- ❖ Your blank presentation will now open. You can pick a theme for your new presentation, which you can change later if you wish.
- ❖ You can give it a name by clicking in the "Untitled Presentation" box at the top left, and then typing in your title. You can click there again to change the title at any time.

* ❖ Google Docs automatically saves your presentation any time you make changes.

How To Import And Convert An Existing Presentation

Instead of starting from scratch, you can also take existing presentations that you have made in other programs, such as Microsoft PowerPoint, and can import and convert them into Google Docs format. Once converted into Google Docs format, you can edit and share the presentation. From the main Google Drive screen, click the upload button next to the "Create" button in the top left.

Now click the "Files..." link

Browse to locate the file you wish to upload and click "Open"

For presentations, you can upload and convert Microsoft PowerPoint presentations of the following file types: .ppt, .pps, and .pptx

To convert the document into Google Docs format, leave the checkbox checked for "Convert documents, presentations, spreadsheets, and drawings to the corresponding Google Docs format". If you uncheck this box, the file will be stored, but you will not be able to edit it.

Click "Start Upload" to import and convert the file

Note: Depending upon how advanced your original presentation is, the converted version may lose some of its formatting and features.

How To Create A Presentation From A Template

Google Docs also offers a large collection of templates to use to begin your documents. This can help save time creating a presentation, such as a photo album, or just to get a new color and design theme.

Go to: https://drive.google.com/templates

The "Template Gallery" will now open. You can choose templates from your school, as well as Public templates from all over the world. You can narrow your template search by choosing document type and category, or by entering a search term. For any template, you find you can click "Preview" to see a full-size preview of the file If you want to use the template, click "Use this template". A copy of the presentation will then open up that you can edit and save for your use

How To Change The Presentation Theme

You can change to look and feel of your presentation by choosing from many pre-made themes. These will alter the backgrounds, font styles, and font colors for all your slides. To set the theme:

❖ Click "Slide" in the top menu bar.

- ❖ Choose "Change theme…" from the drop-down menu.
- ❖ You will now get a window with many theme thumbnail images to scroll through.
- ❖ Click on a theme and then click "OK" to apply it to your presentation.

How To Change The Background For A Slide

If you wish to personalize your presentation more than the default themes will allow, you can insert your background image for any of your slides.

Click "Slide" then "Background…"

You can click "Color" to pick a solid color for the background.

Or you can pick "Image" to add an image from the normal "Insert image" options.

Or you can click "Reset" to go back to the normal theme background.

After making your choice, click "Done" to change the current slide, or click "Apply to all" to change all the slides in the presentation.

How To Change The Layout For A Slide

The slide layout determines the general arrangement of title, text, and space on a slide. Of course, you can always move items around and add more items later, but layouts give you a good starting point. You can change the basic layout for any slide as follows:

Click "Slide" then "Change layout".

You can now choose between six slide layout options: Title, Title and Body, Title and Two Columns, Title Only, Caption, and Blank.

The slide will now update to the new layout.

How To Insert Items Into Slides

 Google Slides allows you to insert a variety of objects onto your slides including Text box, Images, Videos, Word Art, Lines, Shapes, and Tables. Below each of these options is explained.

How To Insert Text Into A Slide

- ❖ Click "Insert" in the top menu bar.
- ❖ Then choose "Text box" from the drop-down menu.
- ❖ You can now click and drag your mouse to create and insert a text box.
- ❖ You can click inside of the text box to enter text
- ❖ You can click and drag the corner handles to resize the text box
- ❖ You can click and drag the sides to move the text box
- ❖ You can delete the text box by right-clicking on it and choosing "Cut"

Advanced: Converting to And From Google Slides

Google Slides has tried to make it easy to convert to and from other presentation software. Here we'll cover the basics of how to convert using some popular programs. Keep in mind that different presentation software has different features, so certain slide elements like animations or color palettes may not convert perfectly. When converting any file type always have a thorough check through your slides for any errors before presenting!

Converting To/From Microsoft Powerpoint: Converting to and from PowerPoint is very straightforward with Slides. It's worth noting that the animation functionality, in particular, is very different in both programs, so it's likely that some animations may be lost in the conversion process. This is something worth checking before presenting!

To download your Slides document as a PowerPoint file, simply click File in the menu bar and hover over Download as.... In the drop-down menu, select Microsoft PowerPoint (.pptx).

Converting from PowerPoint to Slides isn't much trickier. From your Google Drive homepage click the + New button and select File upload, then choose the PowerPoint file to upload from your computer. Once your file has been uploaded, locate it in Drive and right-click. Select Open with... and choose Google Slides.

If you want to insert PowerPoint Slides into an existing Google Slides deck, click File > Import Slides... and then choose a file you have already uploaded to Drive or upload a new one from your computer. Once uploaded, you will then be given the option to choose which specific PowerPoint slides you want to import into your Google Slides deck.

Converting To/From Apple Keynote: Converting Slides to Keynote and vice versa is slightly trickier as it involves the additional step of converting to PowerPoint, as there is no way to convert directly between Slides and Keynote. To convert from Slides to Keynote, click on the File tab in the menu bar and select Download as... then Microsoft PowerPoint (.pptx), and save your presentation. In Keynote, click on File in the menu bar, click Open, then select your converted PowerPoint file in the new window. Your presentation should now import to Keynote. To save it as a Keynote file, click File in the menu bar, then Save.

To convert from Keynote to Sides, open your Keynote, go to File in the menu bar and select Export to > PowerPoint (.pptx). In the new window, select Next > Export. From Google Drive, create a new Slides presentation, then select the File tab in the menu bar and Import Slides. You should then see a new window where you can upload your converted PowerPoint file. From here, you can select specific slides to import or choose all of them by clicking All in the top right corner. When you are happy with your slide selection, select Import Slides.

Converting To/From Prezi: At the time of publishing, there is no way to directly convert Prezi to and from Google Slides. You could use PowerPoint as a vehicle to import your Prezi into Slides. A way to convert Prezi to PowerPoint is to export it as a PDF, then copy and paste each slide into PowerPoint. This is not a very efficient technique, though, and means that some of your colors or slide objects may be corrupted, and all animations would be lost in the PDF conversion process.

Saving Your Work

Saving your work: If you are using the online version of Slides, this means your presentation is constantly being updated and saved as you work. This is why Slides' online version doesn't have a save button. Saving automatically, means you don't have to worry about losing unsaved work if your computer crashes or you accidentally close your browser window.

Saving Your Work To Desktop: If you want to save a local copy of your Slides file to your desktop or a flash drive, you will first have to convert it to a different file type, such as Microsoft PowerPoint. We talk you through how to do this step by step later on.

Duplicating Your Work: There are two easy ways to make a copy of a presentation. From Google Drive, you can simply right-click on any presentation, and choose to Make a copy from the drop-down menu. Alternatively, whilst in a presentation, go to File > Make a copy....

Version Control: If you're used to working with desktop presentation software, you may be in the habit of emailing different versions of a presentation back and forth. This can get confusing, especially when it comes to consolidating changes across versions.

With Google Slides this isn't an issue, because everybody is working from one single document. If you make a change it will be visible to anyone with access to the document. This is very handy, but what happens when you want to revert to an earlier version?

Version History: Slides makes it easy for you to see all previous iterations of your deck and revert to an earlier version if necessary. At the end of the menu bar, after the Help tab, you should see a line of clickable text saying All changes saved in Drive. It may say something slightly different, like the Last edit made 2 days ago, or simply Saving.... Click this text to open up the version history window, where you can view all past edit rounds going back to when the presentation document was first created.

Click on the different dates to see a preview of how the document looked at the time. If you are just looking for a particular slide, line of text, or image that was deleted, you can simply copy it from the earlier version, close the Version History window and paste it into the latest version.

If you want to completely revert your document to an earlier state, click RESTORE THIS VERSION in the top left. If you choose to do this, bear in mind that your current version will be completely overwritten by the version you are restoring.

Naming Versions: If multiple collaborators are working in your deck, the Version History window can sometimes be difficult to keep track of, especially if there are multiple iterations on the same day. To better track the different iterations that you work on, you can easily name different versions.

Offline Working

Using Google Slides doesn't have to require an internet connection. If you use Google Chrome as your browser, you can use Slides offline. This is particularly handy if you want to make changes to a Slides deck on-the-go, or you are due to present in a space without an internet connection.

Setting up Google Slides for offline use: Firstly, make sure that you are connected to the internet and using the Google Chrome browser. In Google Drive, click the icon shaped like a gear in the top right, and select Settings. Under General, make sure that the Offline checkbox is ticked and click DONE. You may see a notification box appear in the bottom left of your screen that says Setting up offline.

Next, navigate to the Slides homepage and click the main menu button (represented by an icon with three horizontal lines) in the top left-hand corner. Go to Settings and make sure that the Offline button is toggled on (to the right). You can now disconnect from the internet and begin working offline!

Google Drive should still load as normal via the Chrome browser. You can open up a presentation and begin making changes. Next to the title of your presentation, you should see a small lightning bolt icon. This indicates that you are now working offline. You can make changes and even present your deck as you normally would when working online. When you are done making changes, close your presentation as normal.

Syncing offline work when you reconnect to the internet: Changes made to an offline presentation will automatically sync when you go back online and open up that file in Google Drive. It's worth noting that, if a collaborator made changes to the online document whilst you were working on it offline, both sets of changes will sync up in the same file. If this happens and you are unhappy with conflicting changes, use the Version history functionality to revert to an earlier version.

Email Multiple Collaborators

One final collaboration feature worth mentioning here is emailing collaborators from Slides. This is handy if you want to send a message to all collaborators. In the File tab click Email collaborators…. Here you can write a message to be emailed to as many or as few collaborators as you want. Simply check the names of the people you want to send the message to in the right-hand column and click Send.

Chapter 6: Google Forms

Google Forms is a survey administration app that is included in the Google Drive office suite and Google Classroom along with Google Docs, Google Sheets, and Google Slides. Forms feature all of the collaboration and sharing features found in Docs, Sheets, and Slides.

Updates And Features

Google Forms is a tool that allows collecting information from users through a personalized survey or quiz. The information is then collected and automatically connected to a spreadsheet. The spreadsheet is populated with the survey and quiz responses. The Forms service has undergone several updates over the years. New features include, but are not limited to, menu search, the shuffle of questions for randomized order, limiting responses to once per person, shorter URLs, custom themes, automatically generating answer suggestions when creating forms, and an "Upload file" option for users answering questions that require them to share content or files from their computer or Google Drive. The upload feature is only available through G Suite. In October 2014, Google introduced add-ons for Google Forms, which enable third-party developers to make new tools for more features in surveys.

What Are Google Forms?

Google Forms is a free form builder tool that enables users to create surveys and questionnaires online to collect and organize information, simple or complex. Forms can be used to plan events, manage registrations, set up a poll, collect contact information, create a pop quiz, and more. Users can send all collected data to a spreadsheet and analyze data right in Google Sheets.

When creating a form with Google Forms, users can select from multiple question types, customize values, and drag-and-drop to reorder questions. Question types include dropdowns, multiple-choice, and linear scales. Users can also use page branching and question skip logic to show questions based on answers. Images, videos (including YouTube videos), logos, and custom logic can be added to forms to send professional-looking surveys and questionnaires to individuals or customers. Google Forms will automatically suggest a set of colors to style the form, or users can choose from an assortment of curated themes.

Responses to surveys and questionnaires are automatically collected and stored within Google Forms, with live response data and charts. Users can analyze entries with automatic summaries, and watch as responses appear in real-time. Raw data can be accessed and analyzed via Google Sheets or other platforms. All forms are mobile responsive, meaning that users can create, edit, and complete forms using any device. Additional users can be invited via email and provided with access for collaboration. Google Forms can be shared with individuals via email, a link, embedded into a website, or shared via social media.

Advantages And Disadvantages Of Google Forms

Google forms are widely used to create surveys easily and quickly since they allow you to plan events, ask questions to your employees or clients, and collect the diverse type of information simply and efficiently. Google forms allow us to include different types of questions such as short answers, paragraphs, multiple selections, verification boxes, pull-down, linear scale, the grid of several options, among others.

Advantages Of Using Google Forms

1. It is a free online tool, that allows you to collect information easily and efficiently.

2. With Google Forms, you can create surveys in a few minutes to ask your clients or collaborators information about your products or service.

3. To start using this tool, you only need a Google account, the same one you need to access Gmail, YouTube, or Google Drive.

4. The interface is very easy to use. Any user with average Internet knowledge can create forms using this tool.

5. The assistant is simple to use. The What-You-See-Is-What-You-Get interface makes it easy to drag and drop form elements and organize them based on actions or events.

6. At the design level, it is possible to choose between a palette of colors, as well as own images as a background.

7. Google forms stores the feedback received so we can analyze it in detail.

8. The forms are integrated with Google spreadsheets therefore we can access a spreadsheet view of the collected data.

9. The general configuration of forms or surveys allows you to collect the recipient's email address and limit the answers.

10. For advanced users, the type of data that can be inserted into a field can be customized using regular expressions. This helps customize the form even more.

11. Google forms allow us to see how the survey will look before sending it over to the recipients.

12. We can send the form by email, integrate it into our website, or send the link via social networks or any other means.

With this tool, you can get unlimited questions and answers at no cost, while other survey tools require payment depending on the number of questions and recipients.

Disadvantages of Using Google Forms

1. It is necessary to have the internet to be able to use this tool.

2. Design customization is very limited. Advanced users can change the design to use the tool for a greater number of purposes.

3. There are some security concerns. The user has to create a good password and protects it to increase the level of security.

4. There are certain limitations regarding the capabilities of this tool. It accepts texts up to 500 Kb; images up to 2 Mb; and for spreadsheets, the limit is 256 cells or 40 sheets.

How To Create And Customize Google Forms?

No doubt google forms tend to be one of the most versatile tools when it comes to the collection, analysis, and storing of information. Here is a complete step by step guide to the secret of making customized Google forms.

Step 1: Visit Forms.Google.Com.

You can open Forms from your Google Drive or Excel sheets too.

Step 2: Choose A Template

The page so opened, offers you the following options. Either you can create your customized form using the blank template or use any of the already available templates from the encircled Template Gallery. For the sake of this tutorial, we will choose a blank form.

Selecting A Template

The first way of customizing a Google Form is by selecting a template from the gallery. Google offers 17 different templates that you can use to quickly set-up the kind of form that you need. These templates are divided into several types:

Personal: These are forms for personal use, such as invitations, person-to-person selling, contact forms, and meeting schedules.

Work: These forms should be used for your workplace or business, like customer feedback forms and job applications for prospective hires.

Education: These are to be used for an educational institution, such as for quizzes or class assessments.

Blank: Use this to start an entirely new form from scratch.

These form templates have preset question types that you can modify or delete if they don't apply to your needs. They make a good jumping-off point for making your templates, as you can customize them further and save them as a custom template. To select a template, go to the Google Forms homepage and click "Template Gallery" at the upper- right corner. Before editing the template, make sure to change the form name at the upper right.

Customizing The Background And Theme Color

Another thing you can do is customize the background and theme color of a form. To do this, when you're in your Google Form, click the palette button at the top right of the page to bring up the "Theme Options" sidebar.

From here, you can select one of the default theme colors available, or use your own with the RGB color picker. This automatically sets the color scheme of your entire form, including accent colors and the default header color. You can also select one of four background colors for your forms. These include a neutral grey color and light, medium, and dark versions of your theme color.

Customizing The Header Image

Another way to customize your Google Form is by changing the header image that appears at the top of every page. This is a great way to visually describe what your form is all about.

Google Forms Header

In your Google Form edit page, go to "Theme Options" again, and select "Choose Image." From here, you can select from a range of stock options Google provides, which are divided into several categories based on usages like "Birthday" and "Wedding." You can also use your pictures. Click Upload to add an image from your computer, or Photos to select one of the images in your Google Photos library.

Changing The Font

You can also change the font of a Google Form, albeit with only a few options available. To do this, go to Theme Options and scroll down to "Font Style." From here, you can pick one of the following:

- ❖ Basic: Sans-Serif Roboto
- ❖ Decorative: Script Parisienne
- ❖ Formal: Serif Cormorant Garamond
- ❖ Playful: Handwritten Patrick Hand

Presentation Settings

Google Forms Presentation Settings

You also can change a few things via the "Presentation Settings" menu. To access this, click Settings at the upper-right corner of the page, then go to the "Presentation" tab. From here, you can change whether or not to have a progress bar, and set a custom confirmation message for your form. The progress bar is a way of showing a respondent how much of the form is left after they finish a question. This is especially helpful for students who are taking a quiz using Google Forms. The custom confirmation message can contain text, links, or contact information. If this is not filled out, it will default to "Your response has been recorded."

Creating Your Templates

This last tip is only applicable if you're a G Suite user, meaning your Google account is linked to your organization. If you and people in your organization frequently have to create surveys with small differences between them, it can be a time-making process to remake them over and over again.

GSuite lets you create custom Google Form templates that are accessible to anyone in your organization. To do this, go to the Google Forms page while logged into your organization account. From here, click "Template Gallery" at the top-right of the page. In the gallery, go to the tab with your organization's name and click "Submit Template".

Select one of the forms in your Google Drive to become the new template. You can then give it a name and select a relevant category like "Reports" or "Trackers". Alternatively, you can duplicate this process in a regular Google account by duplicating one of your existing forms. To do this, right-click the file within Google Drive and click "Make a Copy".

Step 3: Create A Customized Form

Introduction to the provided functionalities:

A. Add A question.

1. With a click on this icon, you can add a question to the existing form. After writing down the question, usually, the answer type is auto-selected. However, if you want, you can change the answer type by selecting the encircled dropdown menu in the above screenshot. It will present you with a list of possible response types. Then provide for required options or so as need be.

2. For each question or the options of the MCQs and checkbox questions, you may add an image by clicking the image icon just next to them. The overflow menu (three-dot icon) on the image, offers you the following functionalities:

- ❖ Aligning the image to left, right, or center.
- ❖ Changing the image.
- ❖ Removing the image.
- ❖ Adding a caption to it.

You can also double click the image in the question segment to re-size it.

However, for the images added corresponding to answers, only an option to remove it is available. Other options available about the question template include:

I. Duplicate The question: The same question template will be created next to the previous one.

Ii. Delete the question.

Iii. Mark It As Required: It will become compulsory to answer this question.

Iv. The overflow menu at the bottom right corner offers varying functionalities depending on the answer type of that particular question. Adding a description is a common feature available for all the answer types.

B) Import A Question.

You can import questions from the previously created forms as follows:

- ❖ Select the form of your choice.
- ❖ Tick the checkboxes of the questions you want to import.
- ❖ Click 'import questions'.
- ❖ Using this feature you may import questions from multiple forms too. This may save a lot of effort.

C. Add A Title And Description.

You may add a separate information segment in the forms where you just put a Title and if required a description too.

D. Add An Image Segment.

You can add a separate image segment which also allows you to embed hover text. (Hover text is the text that is displaced as the mouse moves over the image.) You may resize the image by double-clicking onto it. The overflow menu over the image offers the following functionalities:

- ❖ Align the image,
- ❖ Change the image,
- ❖ Remove the image.

D. Add A Video.

You can add a youtube video to the form. Either search for a particular topic or add the URL of a specific video. You are allowed to add a caption to the video. The functionalities in the other overflow menu are the same as they were in the image segment.

E. Add A Separate Section To The Forms.

It is always a good idea to organize questions related to different topics into different sections. Each section appears on a different page while the respondents fill the form. The overflow menu offers you the option to duplicate, move, or delete the particular section.

Step 4: Customize The Appearance. (Optional)

The color pallet icon at the top of the form unfolds the following :

- ❖ Add a header image: you can either choose an image from a variety of options that Forms offer or browse files from your desktop. Images can be selected from the 'Google Photos' app too.

- ❖ Change the theme and the background color.
- ❖ Change the font style from the four options provided.

Tip: You can choose from the provided theme colors or select a color using its hexadecimal code. The eye icon allows you to preview the form designed.

Note: You can re-order the templates by clicking and moving the six-dot icon at the top of each question/description template.

Step 5: Altering The Settings

In settings, you can set the rules for the respondent to use the forms.

General:

- ❖ Decide whether or not to collect respondent's email addresses: enabling it would set Email as a required field. Then a copy of their responses can also be sent to them.
- ❖ limit the number of their responses: enabling it limits the response from a particular signed in account to 1. This is a key feature when you set a quiz using google forms.
- ❖ let them edit the form after submission. show them the other responses received: this reveals the responses recorded by all the other respondents, it may be shown using some kind infographics or text itself as per the format of the form.

Presentation:

Here you can choose:

- ❖ To show the progress bar: i.e how many sections have been answered so far.
- ❖ To shuffle the order of the questions: especially useful when the form is circulated as a quiz.
- ❖ Show the link to submit another response
- ❖ Change the default confirmation message.

Quizzes:

- ❖ You can choose to present the form as a quiz.

Step 6: Send And Share

By clicking on the send option at the top right, the following box pops up:

- ❖ You can either mail the link to the desired participants directly, share using Facebook and Twitter, or copy-paste the link on other social networking sites. You can also share embedded HTML.
- ❖ You have the added functionality to add collaborators, i.e. the people who other than you can edit and share the forms.

❖ The collaborators can be restricted to the people you have added or you can change the settings to make anyone with the link an editor.

Step 7: Checking Responses

Google Forms provides features to precisely and accurately visualize the information so gathered. This is also why they are preferred to create survey forms.

Google Forms Add-ons

Google Forms is great on its own, but odds are it's still missing some features you want. Forms add-ons let you add extra features to your forms, get customized notifications, turn your form entries into documents, and more.

There's an entire library of add-ons tucked away in the Google Forms menu. Just click the menu, click Add-ons…, then find an add-on you want an install it. You'll then get a new puzzle piece icon in Google Forms, with a menu that lists each of your add-ons.

Most Google Forms add-ons run in a pop-over on the lower right side of your forms editor, and they may also include an options pane that opens in the center of your editor. To open an add-on, just select it in the add-ons menu, manage its settings from its add-on pop-over, and it'll then run in the background automatically.

There's no menu option to manage or remove add-ons; instead, just open the Add-ons pane again, find the add-on you want to remove, click the green Manage button, and then select Remove in its menu.

Here Are Some Of The Best Forms Add-Ons To Get Started:

All Questions Required? adds a simple toggle to make all questions required or not in a single click.

1. Check It Out: Lets you check-in or out items with a form, essentially by rearranging data from one category to another in a spreadsheet. It's a great tool for managing inventory or shared items, or it could be used creatively to, say, approve tasks, or do other jobs where you need to move items between two categories.

2. Choice Eliminator 2: Eliminates options from multiple-choice, list, or checkbox questions if they've already been selected. It's a great way to, say, make a signup form where respondents can each select one day or an order form for limited-quantity items.

3. Data Director: Adds form responses to alternate sheets and sends email notifications based on conditions. You could use it to sort all similar entries into different sheets automatically.

4. Doc Appender: Adds your form results to the end of a Google Docs document instead of a spreadsheet. Each response can be added to unique documents based on form questions, or they each can be added to the same document.

5. Form Limiter: Limits how many times your form can be answered. It can watch for several responses, date and time, or set value in your results spreadsheet, and then will disable your form once that's hit.

6. Form Notifications: Sends custom email notifications to you and optionally to form respondents with details about the form results and a thank you message.

7. Form Publisher: Makes template Google Docs documents, PDF files, or unique spreadsheets for each entry, and then share them via email.

8. Form Field Export: Turns your Google Forms fields into JSON data to import into other form apps.

9. FormRanger: Pre-populates choices in multiple-choice or checkbox questions from a table in a spreadsheet. That gives you an easy way to add questions about data you've already saved to a spreadsheet.

10. Form Recycled: Import questions from other forms to quickly reuse them without copying the entire form.

11. G(Math):   Adds graphs and functions to forms. Type your formula in LaTeX format, or add a function to graph, then insert it as an image into your form.

Chapter 7: Google Keep

Google Keep is a note-taking service developed by Google. Launched on March 20, 2013, Google Keep is available on the web and has mobile apps for Android and iOS mobile operating systems. Keep offers a variety of tools for taking notes, including text, lists, images, and audio. Users can set reminders, which are integrated with Google Now. Text from images can be extracted using optical character recognition, and voice recordings can be transcribed. The interface allows for a single-column view or a multi-column view. Notes can be color-coded, and labels can be applied for the organization. Later updates have added functionality to pin notes and to collaborate on notes with other Keep users in real-time.

Google Keep has received mixed reviews. A review just after launch in 2013 praised its speed, the quality of voice notes, synchronization, and the widget that could be placed on the Android home screen. Reviews in 2016 have criticized the lack of formatting options, inability to undo changes, and an interface that only offers two view modes where neither was liked for their handling of long notes. However, Google Keep received praise for features including universal device access, native integration with other Google services, and the option to turn photos into text through optical character recognition.

Google Keep Tips

❖ Pin your notes to prioritize your most important tasks.

❖ Break up smaller tasks into larger tasks.

❖ Share notes with team members to keep everyone in the loop.

❖ Add annotations to images. Great for creative teams.

❖ Use date-based reminders to keep yourself on track and structure your day.

❖ Set location-based reminders.

How To Install And Log In To Keep

❖ This part's straightforward. Just head to the Play Store, search for Keep and install the app.

❖ Open the Play Store from your home screen or app drawer.

❖ Search for Google Keep and tap the first search result (by Google).

❖ Tap Install.

❖ Following the installation, open Keep and tap the Get started button.

❖ Select the Google account you want to associate with the app.

How To Create And Edit Your First Note In Keep

One of Keep's strengths is that it is very simple to use. Creating a note or editing an existing note is about as easy as it can get.

- ❖ Open Keep from the home screen or the app drawer.
- ❖ Tap the Take a note section at the bottom of the screen.
- ❖ Enter the title and text, and tap the Back button to save the note.
- ❖ Tap the note you want to edit.
- ❖ Tap the desired section to start making changes to the note.
- ❖ Tap the Back button to save the changes.

How To Create And Manage Lists In Keep

Keep allows you to easily create and manage to-do lists. Here's how to get started.

- ❖ Open Keep from the home screen or the app drawer.
- ❖ Tap the List button at the bottom.
- ❖ Set a Title for the list, and start adding items. To delete an item, tap the Delete button on the right.
- ❖ If you've already started a basic text note, you can turn it into a to-do list by tapping the + button at the bottom left of the screen.
- ❖ Tap the + button, and hit the Checkboxes option to turn the note into a to-do list.
- ❖ You can turn the note back into a text note by selecting the Menu button in the top left and selecting Hide checkboxes.

How To Share Notes And Add Collaborators In Keep

Keep has an excellent collaboration feature that lets you quickly share your notes and to-do lists with your friends and family. I use the feature to collaborate with my wife over grocery lists, chores for the weekend, and things to buy for the house. Here's what you need to know about sharing notes:

- ❖ Tap the note you want to share.
- ❖ Tap the Action button at the bottom right.
- ❖ Tap the Collaborator button.
- ❖ Allow Keep access to your contacts.
- ❖ Enter the email address or name of the person you want to share the note with.
- ❖ After adding the collaborator, tap the Save button to share the note.

How To Set Reminders In Keep
The ability to set reminders for notes or to-do lists is one of Keep's most useful functions. The reminders feature works the same way as it does in Google Now: you have the option of creating a reminder based on time or location. Here's how you can easily set a reminder in Google Keep:

- ❖ Launch Keep from your home screen or the app drawer.
- ❖ Tap the note for which you want to set a reminder.
- ❖ Tap the Remind me button in the top right.
- ❖ Set a reminder that triggers at a particular time or a Location.

You can also set recurring reminders for things like shopping lists. Reminders set in Keep will show up in Google Now and Inbox. When you're setting a reminder, you get default options for Morning, Afternoon, and Evening. Here's how to change the default options.

Open Keep

❖ Tap the menu button on the left. It looks like three stacked lines.

❖ Tap Settings.

❖ In the Reminder settings section, tap Morning to change the default time for notification alerts in the morning.

How To Dictate Audio Notes In Keep
In addition to text notes, you can also dictate notes to Keep, with the audio getting automatically transcribed. It is a lesser-known feature that comes in handy when you're taking notes in class.

❖ Launch Keep.

❖ Tap the Speak button at the bottom.

❖ Start recording your note. After you're done speaking, you'll see a text form of the note along with the recording underneath.

❖ Tap the Play button to listen to the note.

❖ How to add an audio recording to an existing note

❖ Adding an audio recording to an existing note is easy.

❖ Launch Keep from your home screen or the app drawer.

- ❖ Tap the note to which you'd like to add an audio recording.
- ❖ Tap the + button at the bottom left.
- ❖ Tap the Recording button and start speaking. You'll see a text version of the recording as well as the audio added to the bottom of the note.
- ❖ You can delete the recording by hitting the Delete button at the right of the audio. Doing so doesn't delete the text, which you'll have to clear manually.

How To Take Images Using Keep

You can easily take photos from within Keep, and extract text from within images.

- ❖ Launch Keep from your home screen or the app drawer.
- ❖ Tap the Camera button in the bottom right.
- ❖ Tap an image from your gallery or tap Take photo to take a new photo.
- ❖ Add a title and text to the image if required.

How To Extract Text From An Image

Want to grab the text from a photo you took, but don't want to manually transcribe from the image? There's a feature for that.

- ❖ Launch Keep.
- ❖ Tap a note with an image in it.
- ❖ Tap the image.
- ❖ Tap the Menu button in the top right.
- ❖ Tap Grab image text.

❖ You can also make annotations to an image by tapping the Pen button in the top left.

How To Add An Image To An Existing Note

If you're looking to add an image to an existing note, it's quick and easy.

❖ Launch Keep from your home screen or the app drawer.

❖ Tap the note you want to add a photo too.

❖ Tap the + button in the bottom left.

❖ Choose to Take photos to take a new photo to add to the note.

❖ Tap Choose an image to add an image from the gallery to your note.

How To Doodle In Keep

Like doodling? You can use Keep to draw digitally, with three modes available.

❖ Open Keep from the home screen or app drawer.

❖ Tap the Pen button from the bottom.

❖ Tap between Pen, Marker, and Highlight tool.

❖ Start drawing on-screen. To go back, hit the Undo button on the right.

❖ Tap the Eraser from the bottom bar to erase your drawing.

❖ Tap the Select button from the bottom bar to select and move part of your drawing.

How To Use Keep As A Bookmarking Tool

Remember Delicious? You don't need a dedicated tool to save bookmarks anymore, Keep does a capable job of saving and organizing your bookmarks.

- ❖ Launch Chrome.
- ❖ Navigate to a website.
- ❖ Tap the Menu button from Chrome to save a link to Keep.
- ❖ Tap Share.
- ❖ In the Share via a screen, navigate to Keep to save the link.
- ❖ Use the Label button to assign a label to the link.
- ❖ Tap Save to add the link as a note in Keep.

How To Export Notes To Google Docs

While Keep has a lot of features, it doesn't offer rich text editing. If you need more robust formatting and editing tools, you can export your note to Google Docs, Evernote, Word, or other word processing services.

- ❖ Launch Keep.
- ❖ Tap and hold on a note to show menu options.
- ❖ Tap the More button from the top right.
- ❖ Tap Copy to Google Doc to turn the note into an editable Google Docs document.
- ❖ If you're looking to edit the document in another word processor, hit Send from the menu.
- ❖ Tap your editor of choice from the Send note menu.

❖ Tap to save the note in your word editor.

You can also save several notes to a single Google Docs file. Just hold down to select individual notes, and then tap Copy to Google Doc.

How To Archive Or Delete Older Notes In Keep
If you no longer need a note, you can easily archive or delete it. Here's how:

❖ Launch Keep.

❖ Tap a note.

❖ Tap the Archive button to archive the note.

❖ Tap the Action menu from the bottom right to access the delete option.

❖ Tap Delete to delete a note.

How To Recover Archived Notes In Keep
If you've accidentally archived a note, you can recover it by going to the Archive tab from the hamburger menu.

❖ Launch Keep.

❖ Tap the menu button (looks like three stacked lines) on the left.

❖ Go to Archive.

❖ Tap the note you want to recover.

❖ Tap the Unarchive button located at the top right corner.

❖ You will be able to do the same for deleted notes, with notes staying for up to seven days in the trash.

- ❖ Tap the menu button on the left.
- ❖ Go to Trash.
- ❖ Tap and hold on the note you want to recover.
- ❖ Tap the Restore button.

How To Sort And Organize Notes With Labels In Keep

Keep lets you add labels to organize your notes. If you're like me and take a lot of notes throughout the day, labels are essential to make sense of the clutter.

- ❖ Launch Keep.
- ❖ Tap the note for which you want to add a label.
- ❖ Tap the Action button in the bottom right.
- ❖ Tap Labels.
- ❖ Add your desired label.

How To Add Labels Via Hashtags In Keep

You can also add labels quickly with the hashtag (#) symbol.

- ❖ Launch Keep.
- ❖ Tap the note for which you want to add a label.
- ❖ Type a #, which brings up all available labels.
- ❖ Add your desired label from the list.

How To Edit And Organize Notes Based On Labels In Keep

You can create, edit, and organize notes by labels with ease.

- ❖ Tap the menu button (looks like three stacked lines) on the left.
- ❖ Tap on a label to show notes tagged with that particular label.
- ❖ Tap Edit to change label names.
- ❖ Tap the Edit button on the right to edit the name of a label.
- ❖ Tap the + button to add a new label.

How To Color-Code Notes In Keep

Along with labels, you can use colors to visually differentiate between different types of notes.

- ❖ Launch Keep.
- ❖ Tap the note for which you want to add color.
- ❖ Tap the Action button in the bottom right.
- ❖ Tap the desired color from the options at the bottom.

Chapter 8: Google Photos

Google Photos makes accessing and sharing your photos from one place easier than ever. That isn't all it's here to do here, it also works very hard to organize all of your photos into albums, and easily manage who can see which photos. These albums let you easily share important moments with friends, as well as keeping more private moments for your eyes only.

❖ Create a new album
❖ Create a shared album
❖ Add photos to a shared albums
❖ Remove access to a shared album
❖ Adjust the sharing settings for a shared album

Create A New Album
Albums help to keep all your photos organized. Some folks like to save albums of specific events so they can find all the photos from their last family gathering, while others prefer to have larger albums that encompass entire seasons or years. It doesn't matter how you prefer to organize your photos, so long as you know how to create an album when you need it. While Google does a good job automatically arranging your photos, these are mostly by date which can make it difficult to find the specific photo you are looking

for. When you create a new album, you'll see the dates of photos in it, along with other pertinent info.

- ❖ Open Google Photos.
- ❖ Tap the overflow icon that looks like three vertical dots in the upper right corner of your screen.
- ❖ Tap Album.
- ❖ Choose the photos you want in your new album by tapping on them.
- ❖ Tap Create in the upper right corner of your screen.
- ❖ Give your album a name.

Create A Shared Album

Shared albums are a unique feature that easily allows you to share your photo with anyone of your choice. When you create these albums, you get to decide who else has access to them. Creation is nearly identical to a normal album, save for the part where you share them with other people.

- ❖ Open Google Photos.
- ❖ Tap the overflow icon that looks like three vertical dots in the upper right corner of your screen.
- ❖ Tap shared album.
- ❖ Choose the photos you want in your new shared album by tapping on them.

- ❖ Tap Next in the upper right corner of your screen.
- ❖ Give your album a name.
- ❖ Tap Share in the upper right-hand corner of your screen
- ❖ Choose who or where you'd like to share the album.
- ❖ Tap Send to invite people to view your album.

Add Photos To A Shared Album

For some shared albums, you may want to add more photos to them as time pass. When you do need to add new content to the albums you have shared with friends and family, it's a very easy process. Additionally, every person that you have shared an album with can choose to receive notifications when you add new photos to this album.

- ❖ Open Google Photos.
- ❖ Tap the album icon at the bottom right of your screen.
- ❖ Tap Shared to open all shared albums.
- ❖ Tap on the shared album you want to add photos to.
- ❖ Tap the photo icon at the upper right of your screen.
- ❖ Tap the photos you wish to add to the album.
- ❖ Tap Done in the upper right corner of your screen

Remove Access To A Shared Album

There are times during which you may end up cutting ties with folks who have access to certain albums. If this happens, or you want to remove someone's access to a shared album, it's a very easy process. This means that no matter who you have shared your photos with, you can revoke that access. This is just another way that Google puts control over your photos directly into your hands. Just remember that you are deleting the shared album and revoking access to everyone who has access to it. Don't get scared though, because all of those photos will still be available from within the app.

❖ Open Google Photos.
❖ Tap the album icon at the bottom right of your screen.
❖ Tap Shared to open all shared albums.
❖ Tap the overflow icon that looks like three vertical dots to the right of the album you want to revoke access to.
❖ Tap Delete share.

Adjust The Sharing Settings For Shared Albums

While sharing an album is quite easy to do, it isn't just a one-click option. You get to decide how much control the folks you share your albums with getting when they see your photos. You can access a link to share photos with, allow other users to add photos to the album, and lets others comment on your photos. You can also see every person who has access to view the photos in this album, and block them if you want to keep the album but remove access for a single person.

❖ Open Google Photos.

- ❖ Tap the album icon at the bottom right of your screen.
- ❖ Tap Shared to open all shared albums.
- ❖ Tap the overflow icon in the upper right corner of the screen.
- ❖ Tap Sharing options.
- ❖ Use the toggle switch to allow others to add photos to this album.
- ❖ Use the toggle switch to allow others to comment on this album.
- ❖ Tap Copy link, to copy a link to share your album.
- ❖ Use the toggle switch to turn off sharing for this album.
- ❖ Tap the overflow icon next to a user's name.
- ❖ Tap Block person, to revoke access to your album.

How Does Google Photos Work?

Google Photos users can upload new photos, view, edit, save, and create new videos, animations, collages, albums, and photos books. You can also download everything, meaning your cloud-based backup can itself be easily backed up onto your computer or external hard drive. For those who don't have a Google device (like the Pixel phone), you can opt to automatically backup and sync your photos and videos as you take them. If you have an Android device, you can limit backup data usage, so you don't run out of data uploading things in the background. You can also set your Google Drive to keep a copy of your photos and videos by going to your Drive's settings, turning on "Create a Google Photos Folder," and clicking save. As photos are added to your account, they will be sorted into categories.

You can easily share photos and albums using the share feature, whether they have photos in them or not. And, provided you have the "backup and sync" feature turned on, you can retrieve your files from the trash for up to 60 days after hitting delete. Or you can always archive photos to get them out of the way, but have them remain searchable within your account.

The Benefits Of Google Photos

These are the main reasons why we consider Google Photos the best cloud storage service going around:

- ❖ You get unlimited storage for free. You can pay if you want your photos stored with the original resolution but you'll probably find the standard high-quality free version is fine. (Images over 16MP are compressed to size, and videos are capped at 1080p resolution). We explain storage more later on.
- ❖ It's packed with numerous features to organize, use, share, and manage photos and videos.
- ❖ It works on all devices seamlessly.
- ❖ You don't need to be overly tech-savvy to use Google Photos. It's fairly intuitive and straightforward to navigate.

❖ Other people don't need to have Google Photos to be able to view the content you share with them (sharing is optional; your content is private by default).

❖ You can archive photos that you want to keep, but don't necessarily want to revisit like screenshots or receipts (find out more about archiving).

❖ It's easy to find a specific photo. You don't need to remember the date the photo was taken. You can search by someone's name, an event, objects, places, text in a photo, or even a map.

❖ You can make movies, animations, collages, and albums to save, share, or embed.

❖ You can access Google Lens to identify objects in photos, copy-paste text from textbooks and documents, translate text in textbooks and on signs, scan QR codes, and more.

❖ You can relive your favorite memories within the app (a very popular feature).

❖ Google Photos has become more than just an app to manage your photos, it's become the home for your life's memories.

Backup And Sync In The Google Photos App

If you take photos on your phone, the easiest way to get them to your Google Photos account is via backup and sync. My phone is set to automatically upload my photos to Google Photos when I'm connected to wifi. It's a good idea to make sure this setting is turned on if you have a limited data plan on your phone (so you don't waste all your mobile data).

To Turn On The Wifi Backup Set:

- ❖ Open your Google Photos app and tap on your profile image (or initial) in the upper right corner of the app.
- ❖ Tap Photos settings (the gear icon).
- ❖ The first option is Backup & sync. Toggle to activate backup & sync.
- ❖ Make sure the two options at the bottom of the screen, "Use cellular/mobile data to back up photos" and "Use cellular/mobile data to back up videos" are turned off.

Google Photos: Awesome New Features You Need To Start Using

Google has been dabbling in photo hosting for years, but it wasn't until it released the revamped Google Photos in May 2015 that it took photo archiving seriously. We can now back up all our photos for free, and even get our images printed in Photo Books. But Photos leverages Google's machine learning muscle to do a lot of other cool things you just need to know where to look.

Favorite Photos

Google Photos makes it easy to save all your photos, but there are probably some you like more than others. When you come across those pics, you can add them to your favorites for easy access in the future. To mark something as a favorite in Photos, just tap to view it and look for the star at the top of your screen.

Tap the star, and your photo appears instantly in the "Favorites" album. This is a special album visible only to you inside Google Photos, but you can still share the items inside it.

Assistant Tab

You're probably familiar with "Assistant" as the voice-activated AI in your phone and Google's smart speakers. However, there's a different Assistant in Google Photos. Just slide over to the Assistant tab to see what it can do. The Assistant tab includes basic housekeeping suggestions like archiving screenshots or receipts. However, it also generates suggested edits to your photos. For example, you might get a fun filtered version of a pic or a little collage of similar images. You might even get a fancy "color pop" image that highlights the subject in color and fades the rest of the photo to monochrome. When you see something you like in the Assistant tab, just tap the "Save" button to add it to your library.

Create Custom Collages

Should you poke around in the Assistant tab, you'll probably see collages. If you want to make your own, there are tools for that in the app. Open the overflow menu and select collage. You can also go over to the Assistant tab and tap college at the top of the screen. You can pick between two and nine photos for Photos to drop into the collage. Unfortunately, you don't have control over which images go in which frames. Google's AI optimizes the composition for you.

Google Lens

Google uses machine learning to catalog all your pics in Google Photos, but you can take it a step further with Google Lens. This image analysis tool goes beyond simply figuring out what's in a photo, and provides actionable information. It's not perfect, but Lens already has some very cool capabilities. To use Lens, find a picture to analyze and expand it to full-screen. Tap the Lens icon at the bottom of the display to turn Google's neural network loose on the image. Currently, Lens is great at identifying books, logos, landmarks, addresses, and some more esoteric things like dog breeds. You'll get useful web links and other actions based on the recognized objects. You can also use Lens to copy text from an image.

Edit Your Videos And Movies

The photos in Google Photos get most of the attention, but let's not forget that the platform also backs up your videos. Google even included some basic video editing tools in the app. These tools come in two versions. When looking at one of your videos, you can tap the settings button at the bottom of the screen. This page lets you rotate and stabilize the video great if you were holding the phone at an awkward angle to capture the moment.

The other editing interface resides in the movie creation section of the app. This is accessible from the overflow menu in the main photo tab. You can choose one or more video (under "Select Photos and Videos"), and then splice them together, trim the ends, and export the project as a new file. Also, don't ignore the automatic movie options in this menu like Selfie Movie, Doggy Movies, and so on. These are generated using Google's AI, so they take a while to process on Google's servers.

Free Up Storage

So, now you've got all your images in Google Photos, do you need them all locally on your phone as well? If you need space, Google Photos makes it easy to clear out the clutter. Scroll up to the top of your main photo tab and tap on the line that says "Free up [some amount of space] from the device."

After confirming the popup, Google Photos will remove all photos and videos from your phone that have already been backed up to Google's cloud. You can still access those images at any time in Google Photos.

Name People

Face detection was one of the earliest examples of Google Photos' machine-learning. From the very beginning, can open the Photos search interface, type in "people," and see groupings of all the faces that commonly appear in your photos. That's neat, but you can make this feature even more useful by attaching names to those faces.

To add names, open the search screen and type "people"—the app should suggest People & Pets. You can also tap the arrow next to the line of portraits under the search box. This opens a series of thumbnails of all the common faces that appear in your Photo archives. Tap a face (or pet), and then select "Add a name" to add a private label. With that done, you can use that label to search for photos of that person.

Quick Select Photos

Google Photos makes it easy to save every photo you take, but that can add up to a lot of photos. If you need to select multiple photos say, for batch deletion, the default way in most apps is to long-press then tap on additional items. However, you can select multiple items in Google Photos without a bunch of tedious tapping.

To select multiple photos, simply long-press and drag up or down. Photos will be selected as you go, and the further you drag, the faster photos will be selected. When you release, you can tap individual photos to add or remove them from the selection. This is great for bulk actions when sharing, creating albums, or just clearing out unwanted pics.

Shared Libraries

A recent Photos addition that shows off Google's machine learning is "Share your library," which you can access from the app's navigation slide-out menu. You can share your entire photo library with someone else, but several options make it a more targeted and useful experience.

The first step is deciding which contacts you want to be included in the share. Once you pick a recipient, the app will ask you to narrow down your sharing parameters. The default setting is "All photos," but you can limit the share to only photos of specific people perfect for parents who want to share photos of their kids with other family members. Just pick your kid's face from a list of all detected faces, and that's it. You can also set a date from which photos will be shared going forward. It can be the current day or someday in the past. Your recipients will get instant access to matching photos as you take them, and can choose to copy them into their library. You can also turn off the shared library at any time.

Sharing Links

When you share a photo in Google Photos, it pops up the standard Android share menu. However, there's a special option hidden in there. Tap "Create link," and you instantly create a link that works for anyone with the URL. This works with multiple images, and there's also a toggle to allow others to add photos to the album at that link.

The link is copied to your clipboard, so you can send it to any app you want. Only those with access to the link will be able to see the album. Should you ever want to discontinue access to that shared image or images, just head over the shared tab in the Photos app? Your links are shown here, alongside regular albums. Tap on the link and use Menu > Delete. This is also where you can add more images to your shared link if you so choose.

Shared Albums

It's easy to share individual images with Google Photos, but you can also share entire albums. This gives you expanded sharing capabilities, and it's much simpler when you need to share a lot of photos.

The first step is simply to pick an album. This can be something you've made yourself manually or an automatically generated album from Photos. This second point is key because Google Photos is great at organizing photos from an outing or event. When viewing the album, tap the share button at the top of the screen. You can use any method you like to let people see the photos in your album, but you should choose the direct Photos sharing option if your friend is also a Photos user.

You can allow others to add photos to the album, and if you connect to someone via Photos, they get notifications when new pics are added. You will always see user icons at the top of shared albums to remind you of who has been invited. Those viewing the album can even leave comments for everyone to see. Like link sharing, you can shut off access to the shared album at any time.

Archiving Photos

Google Photos uploads everything, and sometimes you don't want all the stuff it backs up to be in the main feed. That doesn't mean you want to delete it, though. That's why archiving was added to Google Photos. Google Photos had been getting plenty of attention because it's the perfect place to show off machine learning. That means we'll probably see innovations regularly.

To archive photos, open them or select multiple images at once using the quick-select trick explained above. Then, go to Menu > Archive. Archived photos will remain in your private archive, accessible via the navigation menu. Archived images are kept in any shared albums, but they won't clutter up your main feed. This is great for screenshots and images of receipts.

Chapter 9: Google Calendar

Google Calendar is a time-management and scheduling calendar service developed by Google. It became available in beta release April 13, 2006, and in general release in July 2009, on the web and as mobile apps for the Android and iOS platforms.

Google Calendar allows users to create and edit events. Reminders can be enabled for events, with options available for type and time. Event locations can also be added, and other users can be invited to events. Users can enable or disable the visibility of special calendars, including Birthdays, where the app retrieves dates of births from Google contacts and displays birthday cards every year, and Holidays, a country-specific calendar that displays dates of special occasions. Over time, Google has added functionality that makes use of machine learning, including "Events from Gmail", where event information from a user's Gmail messages are automatically added to Google Calendar; "Reminders", where users add to-do activities that can be automatically updated with new information; "Smart Suggestions", where the app recommends titles, contacts, and locations when creating events; and "Goals", where users enter information on a specified personal goal, and the app automatically schedules the activity at optimal times.

Google Calendar's mobile apps have received polarized reviews. 2015 reviews of the Android and iOS apps both praised and criticized the design. While some critics praised the design for being "cleaner", "bold" and making use of "colorful graphics", other reviewers asserted that the graphics took up too much space. The Smart Suggestions feature was also liked and disliked, with varying levels of success in the app managing to suggest relevant information upon event creation. The integration between Google Calendar and Gmail was praised, however, with critics writing that "all of the relevant details are there

Features Of Google Calendar

❖ Google Calendar allows users to create and edit events. Events have a set start time and stop time, with an option for an "All-day event".

❖ Users can enable a "Recurring" functionality with optional parameters for frequency.

❖ Users can add color to an event for recognition or distinguish the event from others.

❖ Events are viewable in different types of setups, including day, week, month, or schedule.

❖ Locations can be added for easy understanding of an event's place.

❖ Users can optionally set notifications, with options for type (email, mobile push notification) and time.

- Users can invite other people to events; for other Google Calendar users, the event becomes visible in their calendar, and for non-Google Calendar users, an email will have options for "Yes", "No", or "Maybe".

- Privacy settings allow the user to define the levels of public visibility of the entire calendar or individual events. Although the calendar defaults to showing users event times in their local time, users can specify a different time zone for an event.

- Users can enable or disable the visibility of special calendars, including a Birthdays calendar, that automatically retrieves dates of births from a user's Google contacts and displays the dates every year, and a Holidays calendar, a country-specific calendar featuring dates of special occasions

Creating And Managing Calendars

"Add calendar" is an option on the left sidebar. Though you can create calendars for as many or as few topics as you'd like, consider at least setting up separate personal and work calendars. This will enable you to use features such as sharing your work availability with team members while keeping your plans private. All calendars can be viewed simultaneously on your screen so you get a full perspective on your plans, or they can be filtered out so you can focus on the important stuff. Some other ideas for calendars include:

1. **Birthdays:** You can import these from Facebook and other sites, but they tend to clutter up your view. Keeping them in a separate calendar means you can remove them from your view with a simple click.

2. **Workouts:** Keep detailed records or plans for all your workouts right at your fingertips. Again, you can declutter your view with one click if they're in a separate calendar. Check out the goal-setting features described later in this article!

3. **Shared Google Calendars:** Google allows you to request and receive calendars from other users such as family members or colleagues. With a click, you can check if your spouse has free time or see whether your colleague is in a meeting before calling.

You might also want to consider sharing your calendar with others. If you've been working online within the past decade, you've probably used Google Calendar to manage your schedule—or, at the very least, have received an invite from a colleague who uses it.

But as common and straightforward as Google Calendar may seem, it's also packed with a surprising amount of features and integrations that help you manage your time more effectively.

Creating Events

- ❖ Viewing and Accessing Google Calendar
- ❖ How to Create a Google Calendar Account
- ❖ This step is as simple as the directions given above. When you see this screen, simply select "Create an account."
- ❖ From there, you'll have the option to either create a personal account or a business account. Google will subtly tailor the setup and options for your calendar based on the primary use you select.

To add an event to your calendar, click the "Create" button in the top left corner:

You can input tons of information here, and by setting up an event thoroughly, you make things easier for yourself in the long run. Choose which calendar the event is part of, whether it's recurring or one-time-only and so much more.

Customizing Your Calendars

That left sidebar on the Settings page is your best friend when it comes to maximizing Google Calendar's features. Taking a few minutes to explore your options in Settings could save you a lot of time and headaches in the future. We'll go over some of the most important customization settings later on, but it's worthwhile to check out the extent of what Google Calendar can do for you on your own.

How To Import Existing Calendars And Events

If you've already been using a different calendar app to manage your daily schedule, making the switch to Google Calendar is easy and you don't have to lose all your information to do it. Once you have your account set up, you can import all your existing events over to your new calendar with the following steps:

Export data from your source calendar. Usually "Export" can be found in the "File" tab.

Click "Import and export" on the left sidebar in Google Calendar Settings.

Import the file you exported from your other calendar.

Beyond importing calendars, you'll also want to sync up your existing events across platforms. From other scheduling systems to social media, syncing these applications with Google Calendar helps you maintain an accurate view of your commitments and free time.

How To Share Your Calendar

Calendar Sharing is one of Google Calendar's best features. With this tool, you can keep your connections up to date on your daily activities and easily plan around your friends' and colleagues' schedules.

The Process Is Easy, But It Takes A Few Steps To Get Things Set Up.

From the "My calendars" list on the left-hand toolbar, hover over your main calendar (which should be labeled with your name.) Then click the three dots just to the right of the calendar title and select "Settings."

From there, you can navigate to either "Access permissions" or "Share with specific people." By making your calendar available to the public, anyone with your email address can subscribe to your calendar. If you prefer to keep tighter control over who can see your calendar, you can either invite specific people to view it or get a shareable link that you can send to anyone who needs it.

To add someone else's calendar to your calendar view, click the plus symbol to the right of "Other calendars," and select "Subscribe to calendar." If their calendar is accessible to either the public or your shared organization, you should be able to access it by entering their name or email address into the "Add calendar" bar. Otherwise, ask them to invite you directly or send you a link to their calendar.

Remember, you can remove someone else's calendar from your main calendar display at any time. Simply uncheck the box next to that calendar in the "Other calendars" section, and their events will disappear from your calendar until you want to view them again. For more on

How To Get A Daily Agenda From Google Calendar

In the old days (and maybe still in some offices), the day would begin with a cup of coffee and a secretary sitting across from the boss and going through the day's agenda. Google Calendar can do that for you by sending you a daily email with all your scheduled items for the day in any given calendar. (No coffee included you're on your own for that.)

In Settings, click on your calendar on the left. You'll have to scroll down a little bit to get to "Other notifications." Set "Daily agenda" to email, and you'll have it all ready to go!

How To Set Recurring Events

Do you have a staff meeting every Wednesday at 9 a.m.? Or a yoga class every Thursday at 5:30 p.m.? Set up a recurring event in Google Calendar. When you go to plan the coming week, you'll see all the recurring items laid out for you without having to type them out dozens of times.

Another use for recurring entries is getting reminders for things you're likely to forget. For instance, maybe you want to remember to call your mom on the way home from work every Monday. Set up a recurring event in Google Calendar and add a notification to show up on your phone.

Setting up a recurring event is simple. Click "Create" and enter the event, day, and time. Then click "More Options." The pull-down menu labeled "Does not repeat" will give you several choices for setting up a recurring event. You can also choose when to receive a notification to your phone or email (or both, so it'll be really hard to forget to call Mom.)

How To Set Up Meetings

Let's take a look at the "invitation" feature of Google Calendar. When you need to set up a meeting, you can start by checking any of the relevant parties' calendars (see "Creating and Managing Calendars" above for more on sharing calendars.) Once you have a basic idea of your event details, create an event, and click "More options." From there, follow these steps to add guests to your meeting:

Start with "Guests" in the right-hand column, and simply add their email addresses. If they have Gmail, use this address for the best results. You can use the checkboxes under "Add guests" to allow guests more or less control over the event in Google Calendar.

Next to "Event details," click "Find a time." Here, you will see your schedule along with those in your guest list who have shared their calendar with you. This makes it visually easy to see pockets of time when people's availability overlaps.

How To Create Entries With Other Apps

Google Calendar can add events from Gmail, Facebook, and other applications. Some useful ways this comes into play include:

1. Adding Flight And Hotel Info: When you get a reservation confirmation, you can adjust your settings so that Google will import this information into your calendar. When it comes time to find your hotel or terminal, all that information is stored in your calendar.

2. Entries From Gmail: If you're having a conversation in Gmail, and you mention a time and place, Google Calendar will often ask if you want to add it as an event. This can save time and reduce your chance of forgetting the plans you've made with friends, family, or colleagues.

3. Facebook Events: By adding an extension, you can add Facebook events directly into Google Calendar.

4. Smart Devices: Add events to your calendar by using voice control on an Android or Google device. Simply say "Ok, Google," then give the details of the event you'd like to add.

How To Adjust Your Calendar View

When you're sitting down for a planning session, you may want to see a specific amount of time laid out. The easiest way to adjust your view is to click on the View menu on the top right, next to the Settings cog. Here, it's labeled "Week." Choose whichever view best suits you. The menu also lists the keyboard shortcuts, so you can make note of those that you use most often and use a shortcut next time.

Another quick way to change your view is to highlight the days or weeks you wish to see. This can be done on the sidebar by clicking and dragging your cursor over the days. Depending on the length of time you have highlighted, this can bring up a lot of detail at once for only the specific days you're interested in. To get back to a standard view after this, use the pull-down menu or a shortcut.

Want to see more detail on your screen at a time? Click the cog on the top right of your screen and choose "Density and color." Then for "Information density," choose "Compact.

Setting Goals In The Google Calendar Mobile App

Goal setting is a feature only available in the mobile application, but once you get it set up, the implementation can be managed in the web/desktop version as well. This feature uses artificial intelligence to learn your patterns and suggest times to accomplish your goals. Here's how to get started:

Click the plus sign on the app's home page and choose "Goal."

There are several flexible categories to choose from such as exercise, skill-building, friends, and family, my time, and organization. Google Calendar is assisting you in setting aside time for the things that are important to you. After you choose a goal area, you'll be led through prompts about frequency, length, and time of day. Based on the other entries already in your calendar, Google will suggest times that work well for your goal activities. You then can manually change the times it has suggested.

Google uses artificial intelligence software to learn from your activities and selections so that it can make even more helpful suggestions in the future. Some folks may feel concerned about Google knowing so much about them. If data security is on your mind, you can learn about Google's privacy policies and consider modifying your settings to keep your information more private.

Using Reminders And Tasks To Keep On Track

In the web/desktop version, when you click "Create," you have three options: Event, Reminder, and Task. Events are the most common selection, but making use of the other two can help you even more effectively block out your day.

Reminders and Tasks are similar, but they have some important distinctions. Use the Reminder option to add items that need to be accomplished on a particular day but are more of a "to do" than an actual event.x

Reminders are easy to add on either the web/desktop version or the mobile app. Tasks can be used on a mobile device, but they're stored in a separate app called Google Tasks. They don't show up on the Google Calendar mobile app.

Reminders and Tasks can both be marked as "done," but Tasks will transfer to the next day if they're not marked as complete. This can help keep important responsibilities at the top of your mind, especially if you primarily use the web/desktop version of Google Calendar.

Reminders can be set up to repeat (every Monday, for instance), so you don't have to re-enter them regularly. Tasks do not include a recurring option.

Permission Settings

Tip: If you use Google Calendar through your work, school, or other organization, you might not find all these sharing options if your admin turned them off. When you share your calendar with someone, you can decide how they find your events and whether they can also make changes like adding or editing events. Here's what people can do with each sharing option:

Make Changes & Manage To Share

❖ Change sharing settings
❖ Add and edit events

- ❖ Find details for all events, including private ones
- ❖ Find the time zone setting for the calendar
- ❖ Permanently delete the calendar
- ❖ Restore or permanently delete events from the calendar's Trash
- ❖ Subscribe to email alerts when events are created, changed, canceled, RSVPed to, or coming up

Make Changes To Events

- ❖ Add and edit events
- ❖ Find details for all events, including private ones
- ❖ Find the time zone setting for the calendar
- ❖ Restore or permanently delete events from the calendar's Trash
- ❖ Subscribe to email alerts when events are created, changed, canceled, RSVPed to, or coming up

Find All Event Details

- ❖ Find details for all events except those marked as private
- ❖ Find the time zone setting for the calendar
- ❖ Subscribe to email alerts when events are created, changed, canceled, RSVPed to, or coming up
- ❖ Find only free/busy (hide details)
- ❖ Check when your calendar is booked and when it has free time, but not the names or other details of your events.

Tip: Events from Gmail that have the "Only me" visibility setting aren't visible to anyone you've shared your calendar with, even people with "Make changes" access unless you change the sharing settings for the event or the default setting for events from Gmail.

Change Visibility Settings For An Individual Event

Your events automatically have the same sharing settings as your calendar. You can edit the visibility setting for each event, but how visibility settings work depends on how your calendar is shared.

Troubleshooting

If the other person is having trouble finding your calendar, try these steps:

- ❖ Make sure you added the correct email address.
- ❖ Remove the person from the calendar's sharing settings and then add them back. Find the directions above.
- ❖ Make sure they click the link in the email they received. They should check their Spam folder if they can't find it.

Chapter 10: Gmail

Gmail is a free, search-based email (Webmail) service, which is accessible from a Web browser anywhere in the world so long as an Internet connection is present. Gmail was first introduced by Google in 2004 and limited test accounts were made available in 2005. According to Statista, Google's Gmail service has 900 million active users worldwide (Jan-May, 2015). Gmail is a free email service provided by Google. In many ways, Gmail is like any other email service: You can send and receive emails, block spam, create an address book, and perform other basic email tasks. But it also has some more unique features that help make it one of the most popular online email services.

Gmail Sign In

To access a Gmail account, users must first register to create a single Google account to access multiple Google services. On the Google Account sign up page, you will be prompted to enter personal information such as your name, location, date of birth, and mobile number. After creating an account, simply enter the Gmail website URL in the browser's address or location field (https://mail.google.com/) and use the Gmail account by typing in a username and password.

Gmail Powered By Search

The backbone of Gmail is a powerful Google search engine that quickly finds any message an account owner has ever sent or received. When Gmail displays an email, it automatically shows all the replies to that e-mail as well, so users can view a message in the context of a conversation. There are no pop-ups or untargeted banner ads in Gmail, which places relevant text ads and links to related Web pages adjacent to e-mail messages.

Google Accounts

Creating a Google account is needed to access Gmail because it is just one of the many services offered by Google to registered users. Signing up for a Google account is free and easy, and naming your new Gmail address will be a part of the sign-up process. This means whenever you're signed in to Gmail, you are automatically signed in to your Google account. You'll be able to easily access other Google services like Google Docs, Calendar, and YouTube.

Of course, you don't have to use any of these features. You may just want to focus on email for now. However, if you'd like more information, you can review our Google account tutorial, where we talk about some of the different services Google offers and show you how to change your privacy settings.

Gmail Features

Gmail offers several useful features to make your email experience as smooth as possible, including:

Spam Filtering: Spam is another name for junk email. Gmail uses advanced technologies to keep spam out of your inbox. Most spam is automatically sent to a separate spam folder, and after 30 days it is deleted.

Conversation View: An email conversation occurs whenever you send emails back and forth with another person (or a group of people), often about a specific topic or event. Gmail groups these emails together by default, which keeps your inbox more organized.

Built-In Chat: Instead of sending an email, you can send someone an instant message or use the voice and video chat feature if your computer has a microphone and/or webcam.

Call Phone: This feature is similar to voice chat, except that it allows you to dial an actual phone number to call any phone in the world. It's free to make a call to anywhere in the United States or Canada, and you can make calls to other countries at relatively low rates.

Get To Know The Gmail Interface

When you're working with Gmail, you'll primarily be using the main Gmail interface. This window contains your inbox, and it allows you to navigate to your contacts, mail settings, and more. Also, if you use other Google services like YouTube or Calendar, you'll be able to access them from the top of the Gmail window.

Setting up a Gmail account is easy. You will begin by creating a Google account, and during the quick sign-up process you will choose your Gmail account name. In this lesson, we'll show you how to set up your Google account for Gmail, add and edit contacts, and edit your mail settings.

Setting Up A Gmail Account

To create a Gmail address, you'll first need to create a Google account. Gmail will redirect you to the Google account sign-up page. You'll need to provide some basic information like your name, birth date, gender, and location. You will also need to choose a name for your new Gmail address. Once you create an account, you'll be able to start adding contacts and adjusting your mail settings.

To Create An Account:

- ❖ Go to www.gmail.com.
- ❖ Click Create an account.
- ❖ The sign-up form will appear. Follow the directions by entering the required information.

- ❖ Filling in the signup form
- ❖ Next, enter your phone number to verify your account. Google uses a two-step verification process for your security.
- ❖ You will receive a text message from Google with a verification code. Enter the code to complete the account verification.
- ❖ Next, you will see a form to enter some of your personal information, like your name and birthday.
- ❖ Review Google's Terms of Service and Privacy Policy, then click I agree.

Just like with any online service, it's important to choose a strong password—in other words, one that is difficult for someone else to guess. For more information, review our lesson on creating strong passwords.

Signing In To Your Account

When you first create your account, you will be automatically signed in. Most of the time, however, you'll need to sign in to your account and sign out when you're done with it. Signing out is especially important if you're using a shared computer (for example, at a library or office) because it prevents others from viewing your emails.

To Sign In:

Go to www.gmail.com.

Type your user name (your email address) and password, then click Next.

To Sign Out:

In the top-right corner of the page, locate the circle that has your first initial (if you've already selected an avatar image, it will show the image instead). To sign out, click the circle and select Sign-out.

Mail Settings

Occasionally, you may want to make adjustments to Gmail's appearance or behavior. For example, you could create a signature or vacation reply, edit your labels, or change the theme. These adjustments can be made from your mail settings.

To Access Your Mail Settings:

❖ Click the gear icon in the top-right corner of the page, then select Settings.

❖ From here, you can click any of the categories at the top to edit the desired settings.

Adding Contacts

Like all major email providers, Gmail lets you keep an address book of contacts so you don't have to memorize everyone's email addresses. You can also add other contact information, like phone numbers, birthdays, and physical addresses.

To Add A Contact:

- ❖ Click the Google apps button.
- ❖ Click the Contacts button in the drop-down menu.
- ❖ Your contacts screen will appear. Click the Add new contact button in the lower-right corner.

To Edit A Contact:

- ❖ In the Google apps drop-down menu, select Contacts.
- ❖ Locate the contact you want to edit, then click Edit Contact.
- ❖ You can now make any changes you want to the contact

By default, when you send an email to a new address, Gmail adds the address to your contacts. You can then go to your contacts to edit the person's information as needed.

Importing Mail And Contacts

You may already have a contact list from another email address, and it would be a lot of work to re-enter all of this information manually. Gmail allows you to import your contacts from another email account, and you can even import all of your email messages from that account. Several email providers are supported, including Yahoo!, Hotmail, and AOL.

To Add Other Accounts:

Click the gear icon in the top-right corner of the page, then select Settings.

Go to Accounts and click Add a mail account. You can then follow the instructions on the screen to import your mail.

Create And Send Email

- ❖ Open Gmail.
- ❖ On the left, click Plus Compose.
- ❖ (Optional) To change your window size, in the upper corner, click Maximize "or Exit full-screen Exit full-screen.
- ❖ Add recipients and a subject.
- ❖ Enter your message. The email you start writing but don't send is automatically saved in Drafts on the left.
- ❖ (Optional) Add attachments, such as Drive files Insert file using Drive or photos Insert image.
- ❖ Click Send.

Tip: To cancel sending an email, at the bottom of the window, click Undo. This option appears briefly, but you can change how long it lasts. See Undo sending your mail.

See New Email

- ❖ Unread emails are bold. To open an email, click it.

- ❖ By default, replies to emails are grouped into conversations. Keeping all emails together in a thread makes it easier to keep track of them and saves space in your inbox.
- ❖ If you prefer to separate your existing email from future emails, you can turn off the conversation view.

Turn Off Conversation View:

- ❖ At the top right, click Settings Settings and then see all settings.
- ❖ In the General tab, scroll to Conversation View and select Conversation view off.
- ❖ At the bottom, click Save Changes.

Reply To Email

- ❖ To reply to a single email or the last email in a thread, click Reply Reply.
- ❖ To reply to an email within a thread, click Reply Reply.
- ❖ To forward a single email or the last email in a thread, click Forward Forward.
- ❖ To forward an email within a thread, click More Moreand thenForward.
- ❖ To see the previous email in a thread, click Show trimmed content.
- ❖ To forward an entire conversation, at the top, click More Moreand then forward all.

- ❖ To use a Smart Reply, at the bottom of the email, click a suggested reply. You can then edit the email before sending it.
- ❖ Change recipients or subjects

Add And Remove Recipients:

- ❖ From an open email, click a recipient's address.
- ❖ To add more recipients, type their email addresses.
- ❖ To remove recipients, next to their email address, click Remove ".

Edit An Email Subject:

- ❖ Next to Type of response Reply, click the Down arrow Drop down arrow, and then edit subject.
- ❖ Enter a new subject.
- ❖ Save and print attachments
- ❖ When someone sends you an attachment, such as a photo or document, you see a preview of the attachment in the email.
- ❖ See a full-screen view and print: Click the attachment to open a full-screen view. To print, click Print
- ❖ Download an image or save it to Drive: Point to the preview and click Download or Save to Drive
- ❖ You can quickly add images and attachments to your email by dragging them from your desktop to your Gmail compose

window, or drag pictures and attachments from your email to your desktop if you want to download them.

Email Without An Internet Connection

Use Gmail offline to read, respond to, and search your Gmail messages when you aren't connected to the internet. Any email you write, archive, label, or delete while you're offline will be sent or moved when you're back online. When you enable Gmail offline on a device, your messages sync with the browser's storage on the computer you're using. Enable Gmail offline on each device for which you want offline access.

Enable Gmail Offline:

At the top right, click Settings Settings and then see all settings.

Go to the Offline tab and check the Enable offline mailbox.

Note: If you don't see this option, contact your G Suite administrator.

(Optional) Next to Sync settings, choose how many days of email you want to store offline.

Next to Security, choose whether to keep or remove offline data on your device.

Note: If you don't see this option, contact your G Suite administrator.

Click Save Changes.

Turn your vacation responder on or off

Open Gmail:

At the top right, click Settings Settings and then see all settings.

Scroll down to the Vacation responder and select Vacation responder on or Vacation responder off.

If you turned on the vacation responder, enter the dates you're away and add a message. Then, select who should get a response.

At the bottom, click Save Changes.

Open Notes In Google Keep

Open Google Keep: On the right, click Keep Keep.

Tip: If you don't see this option, contact your G Suite administrator.

Add a note or list: Click + Take note or New list.

Edit A Note: Click a note and enter a message. Click Done.

Open Your To-Do Lists In Google Tasks

Open Google Tasks: On the right, click Tasks Tasks. The current list appears at the top, with any tasks below it.

Tip: If you don't see this option, contact your G Suite administrator.

Add A New List: Click the Down arrow Drop down arrow and then create a new list.

Change Lists: Click the Down arrow Drop down arrow and select a list.

Add A New Task: Click + Add a task. To add a new task from an email, drag the email into a task list.

Edit Or Delete A Task: Point to a task and click Edit Edit. From the Edit window, click DeleteDelete reminder to delete a task.

How To Unsend An Email In Gmail

It happens to all of us. You click Send, then realize you've made a mistake. Maybe it was just a spelling error. Maybe you hit Reply all by accident. Or maybe you sent the email to the wrong person, and you don't want that person reading it, because it kinda sorta might contain something super embarrassing. If you use Gmail, you're in luck. Gmail has recently introduced a feature that lets you unsend any email up to 30 seconds after you've sent it. This feature called Undo Send must be turned on before you can use it. Afterward, you'll be able to take back your most recent email in a single click.

To Enable Undo Send:

- ❖ Go to your Gmail account.
- ❖ Click the Settings button in the upper-right corner, then choose Settings from the menu.
- ❖ Make sure you're on the General tab, then scroll down to Undo Send.
- ❖ Check the box that says Enable Undo Send. You can choose a cancellation period of up to 30 seconds.

To Use Undo Send:

From now on, every time you send an email, a small pop-up will appear at the top of the page. To unsend the email, simply click Undo. The pop-up will disappear when the cancellation period is over, so don't hesitate!

Get Add-Ons

- ❖ Customize Gmail with add-ons.
- ❖ On the right, click Add-ons Add. A list of add-ons opens in the G Suite Marketplace.
- ❖ Click an add-on.
- ❖ Click Install.

Time-Saving Email Tips

Many email clients have a variety of helpful features you might not know about. These features are pretty easy to use, and they can save you time and help you to better organize your emails. In this lesson, we'll go over some of these tips and tricks to help you optimize your email experience.

Selecting Multiple Emails

Let's say you have a large number of emails you'd like to delete. It would be fairly time-consuming to go through and individually delete each email. Luckily, most clients have a feature that allows you to select multiple emails. These are usually in the form of checkboxes next to each of your emails. Once the emails are selected, you can then perform any action you want, including deleting, sorting, and archiving.

Keyboard Shortcuts

Most email clients have some set of keyboard shortcuts that can help you navigate your emails more quickly. A fairly universal example is using the arrow keys to scroll through email messages instead of having to click specific buttons. Other keyboard shortcuts (like replying and deleting) will vary from client to client. Below are a few support pages listing shortcuts for some popular clients:

- ❖ Gmail
- ❖ Outlook
- ❖ Yahoo! Mail

If you use an email service other than those listed above, you should be able to find its corresponding keyboard shortcuts via its help page or a quick Internet search.

Creating Groups

If you find yourself sending emails to the same people regularly, it might be a good idea to create a group. Many clients allow you to select various email addresses and save them as a single group. This way, you can simply select the group as the recipient instead of having to select each address. This feature can usually be accessed from the Contacts page of your email client.

Email Filters

When you're receiving a lot of emails daily, it can be difficult to keep them organized. Luckily, various email clients offer a feature called filters, which sort your emails into folders as you receive them. You can create filters that sort your email by various characteristics, including specific senders or recipients, keywords in the subject or body, and attachments. For example, let's say you want to make sure emails from Twitter don't get lost among the rest of your messages.

Can I Have Multiple Gmail Accounts?

Yes, you can have multiple Gmail accounts.

First, let's define some terms:

Primary Inbox: This is the main Gmail inbox most users currently have. It stores all your email as it comes in and only leaves this section when you archive an email or move it to another folder. Multiple Inboxes: These are the new mini inboxes we are creating alongside your primary inbox to organize your inbox into multiple sections based on the email type. They can only be implemented for accounts that do not use Gmail's Promotions/etc tabs.

If you have multiple Gmail accounts, you can pick a primary inbox to send from and merge your secondary accounts to the primary one. Below, we'll take a look at the steps to set this up.

1. Navigate to your "Accounts" settings.

If there's one Gmail account you check more frequently than others, use this as your primary inbox. Navigate to the gear icon, click "Settings", and then click "Accounts" in the top navigation.

2. Add the secondary Gmail account to the primary Gmail account.

In the "Send mail as:" section, click on the "Add another email" link.

Then, type your full name and the secondary email address you'd like to add. You can choose to either check or uncheck the box to the left of "Treat as an alias" is checked"

Checking the box means that emails sent to the secondary email address appear in the primary Gmail account's inbox, which is the goal we're trying to achieve in this example. Once you've checked the box, then click the "Next Step >>" button.

3. Click the "Send Verification" button.

Click the "Send Verification" button to send a confirmation email to your secondary Gmail account's inbox.

4. Enter the verification code.

Once you receive the confirmation email, copy the verification code, paste it in the field that says "Enter and verify the confirmation code", and click the "Verify" button.

5. Navigate to the secondary account's "Forwarding and POP/IMAP" settings.

The next step is to forward the emails from the secondary account to the primary account. Navigate to the secondary account's "Settings" and click the "Forwarding and POP/IMAP" tab in the top navigation.

6. Add the primary account's email address to the "Forwarding" settings.

In the "Forwarding" section, click the "Add a forwarding address button". This is where you'll enter the email address for the primary account. Click the "Next" button and then the "Confirm" button. A pop-up window will appear, you'll click the "Proceed" button, and a confirmation email will be sent to your primary Gmail account.

7. Confirm the forwarding email address.

Copy the confirmation code from the email and paste it into the confirmation code field in the "Forwarding" settings in your secondary Gmail account. Click the "Verify" button.

8. Select a forwarding option.

Finally, click the checkbox to "Forward a copy of incoming mail to ... " and select a forwarding option from the drop-down.

Conclusion

At its essence, Google Drive is a powerful cloud storage solution. But with time, and with the right know-how, it can become an indispensable productivity tool for anyone, from students to business professionals.

Hopefully, this guide was helpful and covered every aspect of what Google Docs can offer, nonetheless, if you still think we missed out on any important feature then let us know, we would love to hear from you. This quick guide to Google Sheets should help you get a running start as you leverage it for your marketing efforts. From more efficient tracking of different metrics to better planning around your content to easier collaboration with your team, this tool can help you make smarter, more data-backed choices that drive meaningful results for your brand.

Google Photos gives you tons of options for sharing and managing the photos that you've taken using albums. You can create new albums, and shared albums, along with tweaking just who can see and interact with the photos that you share. The Google Apps suite is a very good alternative to the more traditional productivity suites (ex. Microsoft Office). Google Apps not only changes the dynamic for interaction between teachers and students, but it can also change the way students exchange with each other. Cloud Computing has numerous benefits, but we shouldn't lose sight of the fact that there is no perfect solution.

Apart from the privacy issues, there is always a risk associated with multiplying the means of communication and the number of platforms used in a college. These applications can simplify your life or make it more complicated depending on whether or not you choose the right tools for the job. Google started by offering a gift economy to organize and make information accessible over the internet. Over time, this developed into an attention economy that gained financial return from monetizing the traffic to its pages through a customized advertising platform that tailors advertisements to viewers. By continuing to offer products and services it uses a free economic model to create an online community of users who continually return to the site (networked economy) to use Google's services.

By presenting simple explanations of the different economic models and applying them to the chosen case study, we have outlined the principles and practices which sustain internet commerce in a way that is easy to follow and understand. Through reviewing multiple online businesses we were able to focus on one that utilized multiple economic models to help explain the similarities and differences between the different ways of conducting business online.

Lightning Source UK Ltd.
Milton Keynes UK
UKHW022117080222
398389UK00011B/2055